2016 SUPPLEMENT TO

HEALTH LAW

CASES, MATERIALS AND PROBLEMS

Seventh Edition

■ ■ ■

Barry R. Furrow
Professor of Law and Director, Health Law Program
Drexel University

Thomas L. Greaney
Chester A. Myers Professor of Law and
Co-Director, Center for Health Law Studies
Saint Louis University

Sandra H. Johnson
Professor Emerita of Law and Health Care Ethics
Center for Health Law Studies
Saint Louis University School of Law

Timothy Stoltzfus Jost
Emeritus Professor of Law
Washington and Lee University

Robert L. Schwartz
Senior Visiting Professor
University of California Hastings College of the Law,
Weihofen Professor of Law Emeritus,
University of New Mexico

AMERICAN CASEBOOK SERIES®

WEST
ACADEMIC
PUBLISHING

American Casebook Series is a trademark registered in the U.S. Patent and Trademark Office.

© 2016 LEG, Inc. d/b/a West Academic
    444 Cedar Street, Suite 700
    St. Paul, MN 55101
    1-877-888-1330

West, West Academic Publishing, and West Academic are trademarks of West Publishing Corporation, used under license.

Printed in the United States of America

ISBN: 978-1-68328-197-9

The authors gratefully acknowledge Allison Goodwin and Kevin Kifer for their research and administrative assistance with this Supplement.

TABLE OF CONTENTS

TABLE OF CASES

The principal cases are in bold type.

2016 SUPPLEMENT TO

HEALTH LAW

CASES, MATERIALS AND PROBLEMS

Seventh Edition

CHAPTER 1

COST, QUALITY, ACCESS, AND CHOICE

■ ■ ■

V. FROM DEFINING QUALITY TO REGULATING PATIENT SAFETY

A. THE NATURE OF QUALITY IN MEDICINE

2. Quality and the Patient Protection and Affordable Care Act of 2010

Add at page 34 at the end of Note 2:

The payment strategies under Medicare provide incentives for hospitals to reduce unnecessary readmissions and otherwise lower their adverse event rates. The problem is that surgical complications lead to higher hospital contribution margins (except for Medicaid and self-pay), since historically the cost of fixing patients after the fact could be billed at the prevailing rates. Hospitals will experience substantial adverse near-term financial consequences of reducing overall complication rate since they will now be financially penalized for readmissions. See generally Sunil Eappen et al., Relationship Between Occurrence of Surgical Complications and Hospital Finances, 309 JAMA 1599 (2013).

C. THE PROBLEM OF MEDICAL ERROR

2. The Extent of Medical Misadventures

Add at page 43 the following new Note 7:

7. Assessing the frequency of medical errors and their contribution to patient deaths continues to be a difficult problem. One recent study concluded that medical errors are now the third leading cause of death in United States, claiming up to 251,000 lives every year—more than respiratory disease, accidents, stroke and Alzheimer's. The authors analyzed four large studies, including ones by the Health and Human Services Department's Office of the Inspector General and the Agency for Healthcare Research and Quality that took place between 2000 and 2008. They used broad categories that included everything from bad doctors to issues such as communication breakdowns when patients are handed off from one department to another.

The authors noted the high degree of variability in evaluating and tabulating data on medical errors—the Centers for Disease Control and Prevention (CDC), for example, does not require reporting of errors in the data it collects about deaths through billing codes. This lack of national standardization in reporting medical errors increases the difficulty in both assessing and reducing such errors. They proposed a national approach to properly fund studies of national patterns of medical errors. Martin A. Makary and Michael Daniel, Medical Error—the Third Leading Cause of Death in the U.S., 353 BMJ i2139 (2016).

The level of severe patient injuries resulting from medical errors has been projected as high as 40 times the death rate. See Frederick van Pelt, quoted in Ariana Eunjung Cha, Medical Errors Now Third Leading Cause of Death in United States, Washington Post (May 3, 2016), https://www.washingtonpost.com/news/to-your-health/wp/2016/05/03/researchers-medical-errors-now-third-leading-cause-of-death-in-united-states/.

Drug adverse events also continue to occur at a surprisingly high rate in spite of initiatives over the past decade in improving drug administration. A recent study of the problem concluded:

> We found that approximately 1 in 20 perioperative medication administrations and every second operation resulted in an ME and/or an ADE. More than one third of these errors led to observed patient harm, and the remaining two thirds had the potential for patient harm. More than two thirds of the harm or potential harm was classified as serious. Thus, there is a substantial potential for medication-related harm and a number of opportunities to improve safety in the perioperative setting.

Karen C. Nanji et al, Evaluation of Perioperative Medication Errors and Adverse Drug Events, 124 Anesthesiology 25, 31 (2016).

E. REGULATING TO REDUCE MEDICAL ADVERSE EVENTS

3. Federal Reimbursement Strategies

b. Federal Quality Incentive Strategies

Add at page 63 following subsection b:

CMS has continued to refine its value-based purchasing strategies, as described in Chapter 10 at page 789. The three broad models are as follows:

- Pay-for-performance—a payment arrangement in which providers are rewarded (bonuses) or penalized (reductions in payments) based on meeting pre-established targets or benchmarks for measures of quality and/or efficiency.

- Accountable care organizations—models of coordinated care in which doctors, hospitals, and other health care providers voluntarily associate to provide coordinated care, with payment tied to overall costs and quality of care for an assigned population of patients. Payment is tied to performance on quality measures and reductions in the total cost of care. This risk sharing model allows providers to choose varying levels of risk in order to gain a share of the savings achieved through improved care delivery, if quality and spending targets are met.

- Bundled payments—payments to health care providers are based on the expected costs for a clinically defined episode or bundle of related health care services, with financial and quality performance accountability for episodes of care.

Cheryl L. Damberg et al., Measuring Success in Health Care Value-Based Purchasing Programs Findings from an Environmental Scan, Literature Review, and Expert Panel Discussions (RAND CORPORATION (2014), http://www.rand.org/content/dam/rand/pubs/research_reports/RR300/RR3 06/RAND_RR306.pdf.)

What are the assumptions on which these payment models are based? What problems can you foresee in using reimbursement models as the preferred regulatory tool to achieve high quality care? What other regulatory strategies might you consider along with, or instead of, payment mechanisms?

CHAPTER 2

QUALITY CONTROL REGULATION: LICENSING HEALTH CARE PROFESSIONALS

■ ■ ■

I. INTRODUCTION

Add at page 89, before Chapter Roadmap:

As noted in the Introduction to this chapter in the casebook, the participation of licensed health care professionals on health professions licensure boards is important for expertise and experience, but professional domination of licensure boards "creates substantial opportunities for anticompetitive conduct facilitated by the authority of the board." One of the licensure areas in which the risk of anticompetitive behavior is especially acute is scope of practice regulation, covered in Section V of this chapter in the casebook. In 2015, however, the United States Supreme Court decided North Carolina State Bd. of Dental Examiners v. Federal Trade Commission, 135 S.Ct. 1101 (2015), a decision that is already working significant changes in the structure and operation of the state licensure boards in many states. (An edited version of the Court's opinions in the case are included in Chapter 14 of this supplement.)

In this case, the North Carolina Board had issued cease-and-desist letters threatening individuals who were not licensed dentists but who were providing teeth whitening services with legal penalties for violation of the prohibition against the unauthorized practice of dentistry. The North Carolina statute did not specifically address the issue of teeth whitening, and the Board relied instead on the state's general and broad statutory definition of the practice of licensed dentistry, which is itself typical of statutory definitions of the practice of medicine and dentistry. (See, e.g., Cal. Bus. & Prof. Code § 2052 on page 113 and K.C.A. § 65–2869 on page 116 of the casebook. See also § 1–20 in Furrow, et al., Health Law (3d ed.)) The use of cease-and-desist letters by health professions boards is a common but particularly pernicious enforcement tool. It threatens serious penalties without going through the procedures required to determine whether the statute was violated and then to impose a formal penalty. The threat alone is usually enough to move providers to stop providing the services in question, because of the financial and reputational risks involved in contesting the board's position, and so it was in North Carolina.

The composition of the membership of the North Carolina Board became a central issue in the appeal to the Supreme Court. The North Carolina dental practice statute required that 6 of 8 members of the Board be licensed dentists engaged in active practice and elected by the licensed dentists of North Carolina. The seventh board member was, as required by statute, a licensed and practicing dental hygienist elected by dental hygienists; and the final board member was a consumer appointed by the Governor. It is quite common, in fact, that the majority of members of a health professions licensure board are members of the licensed profession. As is typical as well, the North Carolina Board was subject to the state's administrative procedures act, and its formal actions subject to judicial review. The FTC filed suit against the North Carolina Board for violation of federal antitrust law in its actions against nondentists providing teeth whitening services; and the Board asserted the state-action defense, arguing that the Board was an entity of the state entitled to immunity.

The Supreme Court's decision in *North Carolina State Board* was the culmination of two years-long campaigns by the FTC to attack restrictive scope-of-practice regulation (see Note 6 on page 130) and to narrow the scope of the antitrust state action doctrine that protects the states from federal antitrust actions. The Court's majority opinion (in a 6–3 decision) does not examine the motives of the members of the North Carolina Board. Rather, it notes that

> Limits on state-action immunity are most essential when the State seeks to delegate its regulatory power to active market participants, for established ethical standards my blend with private anticompetitive motives in a way difficult even for market participants to discern. Dual allegiances are not always apparent to an actor. In consequence, active market participants cannot be allowed to regulate their own markets free from antitrust accountability.

The issue, then, is the structure of the board and not any specific bad behavior of its individual members. Because a "controlling number" of the Board's members were "active market participants" in the Court's view, the Board was not entitled to state-action immunity unless its actions were actively supervised by the state itself. This holding leaves the states with the choice to either restructure the membership of their boards or to put procedures in place to assure supervision of board actions by state actors outside of the board itself. The Court's opinion does not provide clear definitions of a "controlling number;" "active market participants;" or "active supervision." As to active supervision, the opinion says that the standard is to be "flexible and context-dependent" and need not entail "day-to-day involvement in an agency's operation." The opinion does list a few minimal characteristics required of active supervision: the "supervisor" must review the substance of the decision and not just the procedure followed; must have the power to veto or modify decisions; must exercise actual review rather than merely having the potential for doing so; and cannot be an active market participant.

The FTC issued guidance following the Court's decision that provides the FTC's fairly aggressive interpretation of the application of the decision to professional licensure boards. FTC, FTC Staff Guidance on Active Supervision of State Regulatory Boards Controlled by Market Participants (2015). Following *North Carolina State Board*, most states are considering restructuring the operations of their health professional licensure boards to assure that the boards will fall within state-action antitrust immunity. Thus far, states do not seem to be moving in the direction of removing professionals who are active practitioners from board membership. There are a variety of other approaches being considered and implemented, however. These include establishing a supervisory review board for the health professions boards which does not have active market participants as members (or at least not a controlling number) and which have the requisite authority to act as a supervisor. A less complex tool is the appointment of an officer of the state (such as someone from the state's attorney general's office or from another state agency) to act as supervisor. Finally, the lowest hanging fruit is to restrict the use of cease-and-desist letters where there is no specific statutory prohibition of the unlicensed provision of the service in question. The boards typically have access to more formal rulemaking processes, which they should use instead for interpreting general statutory provisions, producing a process that generally would involve review by bodies or officers that would qualify as active supervision.

Although *North Carolina State Board* involved a scope of practice issue, the implications of the decision extend into all of the areas of health professional board activities covered in this chapter in the casebook. In fact, one of the earliest cases to apply *North Carolina State Board* involved an action by the Texas medical board requiring that a physician meet a patient face-to-face prior to prescribing any medication, effectively prohibiting the practice of telemedicine. (See Note 7 on page 101 of the casebook. See also § 1–6(a)(2) of Furrow, et al., Health Law (3d ed.)) In a suit by a telemedicine firm alleging violations of federal antitrust law, the District Court denied the board's motion for dismissal based on state-action immunity for lack of active supervision of the board's activity. Teladoc, Inc. v. Texas Medical Board, No. 1-15-CV-343 RP, 2015 WL 8773509 (W.D. Tex. Dec. 14, 2015), on appeal to the Fifth Circuit. (But see, Rivera-Nazario v. Corporacion del Fondo del Seguro del Estado, No. CV 14-1533 (JAG), 2015 WL 9484490 (D.P.R. Dec. 29, 2015) granting immunity under state action.) Of course, the Supreme Court's narrowing of state-action antitrust immunity has tentacles that reach broadly beyond the area of professional licensure and discipline. See discussion in Chapter 14 of this supplement.

CHAPTER 3

QUALITY CONTROL REGULATION OF HEALTH CARE INSTITUTIONS

■ ■ ■

II. CONTEXT

A. DIFFERENCES BETWEEN HOSPITALS AND NURSING HOMES

Add at page 140 at the bottom of the page:

Changes in Medicare payment methodology (as described in Chapter 10 of the casebook and this supplement) are significant for long-term care providers, and drive provider behaviors, even though Medicare does not pay for residents receiving what people generally refer to as "nursing home care." Although Medicare pays only for very limited nursing home services, focusing on shorter stay post-hospitalization rehabilitative care, Medicare payments generally produce a greater margin of payment over cost than do payments from Medicaid. Most skilled nursing facilities work hard to assure that they have a substantial revenue stream from Medicare eligible services. Medicare payment methodologies, such as value-based purchasing and bundling, are migrating to long-term care. This migration to long-term care occurs both through the ripple effects of changes in Medicare hospital payment methodologies and in the direct application of outcomes oriented payments to skilled nursing facilities and other long-term-care providers. Both are beginning to have significant effects on care patterns and quality measures in long-term care.

Decades of experience with Medicare payment systems have demonstrated the impressive capacity of the health care industry to shift to more profitable sites of care when one site has encountered restrictive payments. So, for example, when the DRG methodology restricted payments for hospital care, hospitals moved patients earlier to lower levels of care, often in designated units within the hospital entity itself, including service lines like outpatient surgery or sub-acute units, or to post-hospitalization rehabilitation services within skilled nursing facilities or to home care. Although this reduced hospital costs, it didn't necessarily eliminate those costs and instead shifted them to other Medicare-reimbursed services. Any transfer of a patient from one provider or entity to another also creates challenges for coordination or continuity of care and can produce poor quality. Tying payment for services across different sites of care should reduce strategic payment-related transfers and should increase inter-site collaboration and coordination of care. Under the ACA, penalizing hospitals that exceed expected rates of hospital readmissions after discharge is intended, in part to drive care coordination, one of the key aims of the ACA. See page 61 in Chapter 1 of the casebook. Even without CMS action directly applicable to SNFs, most skilled nursing facilities already are measuring and trying to improve their rates of hospital readmissions because hospitals are the primary source of nursing home admissions for Medicare post-hospital rehabilitation services.

In a more direct approach to tying quality and payment in long-term care, the Improving Medicare Post-Acute Care Transformation (IMPACT) Act of 2014 (P.L. 113–185) requires CMS to develop a system to link payment to quality measures for all post-acute care (PAC) providers in all care settings, including skilled nursing facilities. In setting standards across all facilities providing post-hospitalization care, IMPACT is intended to promote safer transitions in care. CMS has included IMPACT requirements in its comprehensive revision of Medicare and Medicaid standards for nursing homes. See note for Page 152 below. CMS has also issued final and proposed rules to move toward "value-based purchasing" (VBP) for Medicare payments for skilled nursing facilities by 2018 as required by the Protecting Access to Medicare Act of 2014 (PAMA) (P.L. 113–93). The goal of VBP is to create incentives for better outcomes by shifting to a payment method that creates penalties and rewards for particular outcomes. PAMA requires that the quality measure for value-based payments be the overall rate of readmissions and the rate of potentially preventable readmissions of SNF patients to the hospital within 30 days of discharge from the hospital. CMS has issued proposed rules to specify the standards for SNF potentially preventable hospital readmissions. 81 Fed. Reg. 24230–01 (Apr. 25, 2016).

Add at page 141 at the last paragraph:

CMS has issued proposed regulations to govern the use of binding arbitration clauses in long-term care facilities. The proposed regulations require that admission not be conditioned on agreement to binding arbitration; that the clause be explained in language that the resident understands and include certain required information; that persons affiliated with the facility acting as guardian or representative of the resident cannot give binding consent to such clauses; and that arbitration must occur before a neutral arbitrator in a venue convenient to the resident. The proposed regulations prohibit confidentiality clauses that often accompany binding arbitration so that the resident or others can report concerns to state and federal agencies even for issues subject to arbitration. Finally, the proposed rule asks for comments on whether binding arbitration clauses should be prohibited in skilled nursing facilities. 80 Fed. Reg. 42168 (July 16, 2015).

Add at page 143 at the end of *Problem: Designing Market-Driven Quality Initiatives for Nursing Homes***:**

The Improving Medicare Post-Acute Care Transformation (IMPACT) Act of 2014 (P.L. 113–185) requires the development and application of quality measures across all providers of post-acute (i.e., post-hospitalization) care. The required quality metrics include pressure ulcers, changes in functional status, changes in cognitive status, and special services. IMPACT requires public reporting of performance on certain measures across all settings. Reportable measures include hospitalization, rehospitalizations, pressure ulcers, medication reconciliation, falls, patient preferences, and Medicare cost per beneficiary. Public reporting of these specific measures represents a significant expansion of reporting currently available on Nursing Home Compare. Implementation of IMPACT is to begin in late 2018.

III. REGULATORY PROCESS

B. STANDARD SETTING, INSPECTION, AND SANCTIONS

1. Standard Setting

Add at page 152 at the end of Note 2:

HHS has issued a notice of proposed rulemaking for a comprehensive revision of regulations under the Medicare and Medicaid statutes for long-term-care providers. 80 Fed. Reg. 42168 (July 16, 2015). The agency supports its effort to do this complete overhaul for several reasons. The regulations have not been comprehensively reviewed and revised since they were put in place in 1991 following OBRA 1987 (the NHRA). The nursing home population has changed and become more clinically complex. Some of the higher complexity and acuity is attributable to nursing homes caring for more post-acute residents requiring rehabilitation. In addition, however, the development of independent living and assisted living options have meant that healthier persons who in the past would have resided in nursing homes live in these less restrictive environments, leaving the nursing homes with more debilitated and dependent residents. Finally, nursing homes now have a much higher proportion of their residents who require significant behavioral health support, especially for those with dementia. Practice standards also have changed and the evidence base for improving quality of care has grown. Finally, the revised regulations would implement requirements adopted in the ACA, including the adoption of the QAPI (Quality Assurance and Performance Improvement) process; the requirement of intra-facility compliance and ethics committees; and support for person-centered care or culture change. (The ACA requirements are described in Note 3 on page 152 and in the Note: CMS

Quality Improvement Initiatives on page 172 of the casebook). The proposed regulations also address the requirements of the Improving Medicare Post-Acute Care Transformation (IMPACT) Act of 2014, described above.

Some of the proposed revisions merely update language or place existing provisions in different sections, but the proposed regulations also make significant changes to many of the standards included in the current regulations. Some of the proposed rules specify or increase requirements for staff training or staff qualifications, and these are addressed in the addendum to the Setting Standards for Staffing Problem, below. Many of the proposed revisions occur in sections addressing residents' rights, and those revisions are described in the addendum to the Residents' Rights Problem, below. Other revisions establish new obligations on the part of facilities. For example, the proposed regulations add new requirements for behavioral health services (§ 483.40) as well as sections for the QAPI (§ 483.75) and compliance/ethics (§ 483.85) requirements of the ACA.

Finally, in its comments to the proposed regulations, HHS recognizes that most long-term care providers care for both short stay, post-acute residents (with care paid for and regulated by Medicare's skilled nursing facility (SNF) program) and longer stay residents (with care paid for privately or paid for and regulated by Medicaid's nursing facility (NF) program). The majority of nursing homes in the U.S. participate in both programs, in effect operating two very different care regimes in one facility. HHS notes:

> While CMS is engaged in the issues around long stay nursing home residents, we do not have enough verifiable information to propose specific changes to the regulations specifically applicable to long-stay situations at this time. We solicit comments on how the requirements could acknowledge the special needs of the long stay resident. In addition, because we also received comments regarding the need to specifically address the needs of short stay residents, we solicit comments on how the requirements could acknowledge the special needs of short stay residents. Nursing facility providers describe the challenges of serving these two rather different populations in a single model of care. We are particularly interested in any suggestions to improve existing requirements, within the authority of [the] existing statute, where they make serving one or the other population difficult or less effective.

This is a very telling comment that reveals exactly how much nursing home care has changed since OBRA 1987 (the NHRA) when the focus was on improving the quality of life as well as quality of care of residents (not patients) of nursing "homes."

Add at page 154 after the fourth paragraph in *Problem: Setting Standards for Staffing*:

HHS proposed regulations create a new section (§ 483.95) that describes the required components for staff training programs, which are applicable to employees, contractors, and volunteers. 80 Fed. Reg. 42168 (July 16, 2015). These include the mandated training in abuse and neglect adopted in the ACA, but also include training in effective communication, residents' rights, QAPI, infection control, compliance and ethics, and behavioral health. The proposed regulations also adopt minimum credentialing in some areas. As one example, the proposed rule specifies that a "qualified dietitian" (required under current regulations) be one who is registered by the Commission on Dietetic Registration of the Academy of Nutrition and Dietetics or who meets state licensure or certification requirements. An individual currently serving in the role of the "qualified dietitian" but without these credentials would have 5 years to meet this standard.

Generally, however, the proposed rules require staffing that is targeted to the specific patient population and scope of services of the facility. Facilities would be required to perform at least annually a "facility-wide assessment" that accounts for the facility's specific population in terms of numbers, levels of care, staff competencies required to provide care, and cultural aspects related to the population. The assessment must also identify the resources, in terms of equipment and personnel, required for quality care and include a facility-based risk assessment and a community-based risk assessment. (§ 483.70)

Add at page 155 to the beginning of *Problem: Resident's Rights*:

HHS has issued proposed regulations that would make some significant changes in the current Residents' Rights regulations. 80 Fed. Reg. 42168 (July 16, 2015). The proposed regulations reorganize the current Residents' Rights provisions so that some appear in a new section on Facility Responsibilities (§ 483.11). As a general matter, the proposed regulations move more firmly toward a more patient-centered care model, with an emphasis on individualized care plans, services, and choice. Two of the areas relevant to this Problem are addressed in the proposed regulations in a way that is worth noting.

First, the current regulation on restraints (at page 159 of the casebook) adds nothing to the statutory language. Instead, CMS includes more detailed guidelines in its State Operations Manual (excerpted at page 159). The proposed regulations expand the treatment of physical restraints by specifically addressing the use of bed rails, identifying when they may be used and specifically what standards they must meet to assure that the bed rails don't injure the resident. (§ 483.25(d)(2)). In addition, the proposed regulations would require facilities to provide extensive professional pharmacy review of resident medications with special emphasis on psychotropic drugs. (§ 483.45). Finally, a new section on Behavioral Health Services (§ 483.40) would require that a facility have adequate staff with competencies and skill sets in "non-pharmacological interventions" to provide care to persons with mental conditions including dementia. CMS and OIG already focus on the use of chemical restraints in the form of medications to control behavioral issues in nursing home restraints and have over the past several years monitored their use as potential violations of statutory standards on restraints.

The proposed regulations address transfer and discharge in a section entitled "Transitions of Care." (§ 483.15). The proposed regulation move from the solely rights-based approach evident in the statutory excerpt on page 157 to a more clinically oriented approach. This is intended to meet current policy goals of improving quality of care by assuring continuity of care and by reducing unnecessary hospital readmissions. The new section includes restrictions on admission agreements as well as requirements for transfer and discharge. The restrictions on the reasons for transfer or discharge in the proposed regulations remain those identified in the statute at page 157 in the casebook, although the proposed rules restrict discharge for nonpayment to require that residents not be discharged until the third-party payer has reviewed an application and refused payment or the resident has refused to apply for Medicare or Medicaid payment. The proposed regulation adds significant requirements for assuring continuity of care to the transferred/discharged resident. For example, the proposed regulation requires that very detailed documentation of the resident's medical history, current diagnoses, laboratory tests, and medications, among other information be provided to the receiving facility. It also requires that the facility provide and document that the facility has provided an orientation to the resident prior to transfer or discharge. The proposed regulations also requires that a resident be assessed in person by a physician, PA, or NP prior to transfer to a hospital, except in emergency situations. (§ 483.30). In the case of discharge, the proposed regulations require extensive discharge planning which begins with the assessment performed at admission and is a continuous process thereafter. The provision appears in the section titled "Comprehensive Person-Centered Care Planning." (§ 483.21).

IV. PRIVATE ACCREDITATION OF HEALTH CARE FACILITIES

Add at page 175 at the bottom:

HHS has issued a Final Rule revising its regulations to meet the requirements of the Medicare Improvements for Patients and Providers Act (MIPPA) (P.L. 110–275) regarding deemed status for health facilities accredited by approved accrediting organizations. 80 Fed. Reg. 29796 (May 22, 2015). The regulations tighten the review, approval, and oversight process for national accrediting organizations (AOs) seeking deemed status for their accredited health care providers. As a matter of general direction, the new Final Rule brings accreditation organizations seeking deemed status into a closer relationship with CMS and empowers CMS to exercise more direct oversight over the accrediting organizations and the individual facilities relying on deemed status. HHS reports that 21 accreditation programs provided by 9 national accrediting organizations have been approved by CMS as qualifying accredited facilities for deemed status.

The statute requires CMS to approve accrediting organization programs meeting federal standards for deemed status for several types of health care facilities, but only permits CMS in its discretion to do so for skilled nursing facilities. Many believed that the agency's earlier proposed rules under MIPPA (78 Fed. Reg. 20564 (April 5, 2013)) indicated an interest on the part of CMS to adopt deemed status for accredited skilled nursing facilities, a proposal that continues to be controversial as it was when first proposed in 1981. In responding to concerns that CMS intended to begin approving AOs for SNFs, the agency responded:

> [W]e proposed revisions to the regulations to recognize the technical possibility that at some future date an AO may choose to submit an application for our approval of a Medicare SNF accreditation program.

> However, we emphasize that it was not the intent of our proposed revisions to signal any interest on our part in receiving AO applications for approval of a Medicare long term care facility accreditation program. . . .

> . . . [I]n our recent annual reports to Congress on the performance of AOs with CMS-approved accreditation programs we have continued to identify persistent disparities in identification of significant deficient practices by AOs when compared to SAs [State Agencies] through the validation survey program. We continue to work with the AOs through our oversight activities to identify and address the sources of these disparities, but this more recent evidence is consistent with [our] position [rejecting deemed status for SNFs].

> Further, the commenters raise important issues about the apparent contradictions between section 1865 of the [Medicare Improvements for Patients and Providers Act] prohibition on disclosure of most accreditation surveys and other statutory provisions that require disclosure of all long term care facility surveys. [Ed. Note: as in the Nursing Home Transparency and Improvement Act]. Should we ever receive an application from an AO seeking our approval of a Medicare SNF accreditation program, these and other similar issues would weigh very heavily in any decision on our part whether to exercise our discretion to disapprove a Medicare SNF accreditation program, regardless of whether the AO's application suggested that its requirements met or exceeded the Medicare SNF requirements.

The final regulation revised the proposed rule in response to negative comments to clarify that CMS "may disapprove a SNF accreditation application based either on its failure to provide reasonable assurances to CMS regarding the equivalence of its accreditation program, or based on our decision to exercise our discretion to not approve the AO's application for any other reason."

CHAPTER 4

THE PROFESSIONAL–PATIENT RELATIONSHIP

∎ ∎ ∎

III. INFORMED CONSENT: THE PHYSICIAN'S OBLIGATION

B. THE LEGAL FRAMEWORK OF INFORMED CONSENT

3. Disclosure of Physician–Specific Risk Information

Add at page 225 the following material to the end of *Problem: Content for Physician Compare*:

As of 2016 both groups and individual providers will be posted on Physician Compare. In addition, CMS is releasing all of the Physician Quality Reporting System (PQRS) data for measures on which a physician reports. Information will be available from the Value-Based Payment Modifier (VM) program, based on both the quality and cost of care a physician provides to Medicare beneficiaries. Physician Compare also will include all measures reported by the Medicare Shared Savings Program, as well as indicating physicians who support the U.S. Department of Health and Human Services Million Hearts initiative. Finally, Physician Compare will report utilization data generated from Medicare Part B claims using Healthcare Common Procedure Coding System (HCPCS) codes to describe services and procedures rendered.   https://www.cms.gov/Medicare/Quality-Initiatives-Patient-Assessment-Instruments/physician-compare-initiative/About-Physician-Compare-An-Overview.html.

The home page for Physician Compare is: https://www.medicare.gov/physiciancompare/search.html.

Physician participation in these quality activities is voluntary. CMS says on its website that "[T]here are many reasons why health care professionals and group practices may not participate in CMS Quality Programs even though they're committed to providing high-quality health care. Participation in CMS Quality Programs shows a commitment to quality care. But, participation alone does not mean quality care has been achieved. Showing a commitment to quality is the first step in achieving quality care."

The American Medical Association and other specialty societies complain that the site is confusing and misleading, and that many physicians do not participate in the quality reporting.

Pick a physician whom you or your family know, and use the Physician Compare website to see what information is available. Does it provide useful information in helping you select a physician for the first time? What would you like to see on a website to add value to your shopping for a physician?

5. Disclosure of Financial Conflicts of Interest

Add at page 253 the following material to the end of *Note: Physician Payment Sunshine Act*:

The Sunshine Act raises a number of interesting questions. The first is whether patient awareness of physician receipt of industry payments affects patient trust in their physicians, or how they shop for physicians generally. One study found that patients viewed doctors favorably who received payments for consulting with drug companies, while they saw physicians who had no such contacts as inexperienced. Patients also reacted significantly more negatively to a doctor who received a large payment (defined as $4153) compared to a doctor receiving either a small payment or no payment at all. The authors concluded that " . . . assuming a good faith justification is present, patients, it appears, are likely to interpret many of these financial relationships in a positive light." The authors also noted that very few patients consulted the Open Payments website. Joshua E. Perry, Dena Cox, and Anthony D. Cox, Trust and Transparency: Patient Perceptions of Physicians' Financial Relationships with Pharmaceutical Companies, 42 J. Law, Medicine & Ethics 475, 488 (2014).

A second question is whether the assumptions of the Act are realistic. Are physician prescribing patterns in fact affected by payments from industry? If they are, even at low levels of payment, should this affect patient trust in their physicians? A recent study quantified the association between industry payments and physician prescribing patterns. The authors' findings were quite striking. They found that, compared to the receipt of no industry-sponsored meals, "receipt of a single industry-sponsored meal, with a mean value of less than $20, was associated with prescription of the promoted brand-name drug at significantly higher rates to Medicare beneficiaries." Furthermore, the relationship was dose-dependent: more and costlier meals led to greater increases in physician prescribing of the promoted drug. Colette DeJong et al., Pharmaceutical Industry-Sponsored Meals and Physician Prescribing Patterns for Medicare Beneficiaries Colette DeJong et al., JAMA Intern Med E7 (2016).

Is a website-based disclosure approach the best regulatory strategy for reducing physician prescribing abuses? Should we consider a new regulatory approach to physician receipt of money and meals from industry? How about a total prohibition on payments?

IV. CONFIDENTIALITY AND DISCLOSURE IN THE PHYSICIAN–PATIENT RELATIONSHIP

B. FEDERAL MEDICAL PRIVACY STANDARDS

Add at page 278 the following new Note 7:

7.   Under HIPAA, any disclosure of details of medical procedures performed or personal information about patients in website comments is a violation of patient privacy. Even when no PHI is disclosed in the comments, healthcare providers breach HIPAA Rules simply by confirming that the commenter is one of their patients. Even when a patient posts a comment about a physician or other healthcare provider, they have not given their permission for any information about them to be disclosed. That includes their status as a patient of a particular healthcare provider.

The proliferation of consumer feedback sites such as YELP offers patients the chance to praise their physicians, and to complain about them. Negative reviews have triggered provider responses to the negative comments, in violation of HIPAA rules. Health Providers Violate HIPAA Responding to Negative YELP Reviews, HIPAA Journal (June 1, 2016). http://www.hipaajournal.com/. A ProPublica report based on access to around 1.7 million Yelp reviews of healthcare providers found dozens of examples of providers who responded to comments, often disclosing patients' protected health Information in the process. In one case, a dentist responded to a patient's comment about an alleged unnecessary tooth extraction with clinical details about the patient, such as "Due to your clenching and grinding habit, this is not the first molar tooth you have lost due to a fractured root."

The Office for Civil Rights (OCR) and state attorneys general can issue heavy fines for HIPAA violations and breaches of patient privacy. In 2013, Shasta Regional Medical Center agreed to pay the OCR $275,000 after the impermissible disclosure of a patient's protected health information to the media.

CHAPTER 5

LIABILITY OF HEALTH CARE PROFESSIONALS

■ ■ ■

VI. DAMAGE INNOVATIONS

**Add at page 415 following the *Notes and Questions* the following
new section C:**

C. THE AFFORDABLE CARE ACT AND ITS POTENTIAL EFFECT ON COLLATERAL SOURCE RULE DAMAGE LIMITATIONS

Tort defendants have begun to argue, and some courts have recognized, that the ACA may provide a basis to substantially limit plaintiffs' claims for future damages. The ACA, by providing for mandatory insurance coverage, including requirements for many "essential health benefits", and setting annual cost limits that an insured may pay for such coverage, arguably redefines both the prospect of future coverage and the calculation of what such coverage may cost to a plaintiff claiming future medical damages.

Plaintiffs rely on the collateral source rule—still the law in many states—as a basis to argue that evidence of prospective ACA coverage is inadmissible. The collateral source rule prohibits the admission of evidence that the plaintiff or victim has received compensation from some source other than the damages sought against the defendant. Critics of the collateral source rule argue that an injured person should not receive a double recovery. Proponents note that deterrence is best served by imposing the full cost of negligent behavior on the defendant as the at-fault party, in order to reinforce the standard of reasonable care that all members of a society should adhere to. A second justification is that an injured person should not receive reduced compensation for injuries because he or she was prudent enough to purchase insurance prior to the injury. And a third justification is that an award of full damages, including future medical costs, provides a more adequate fund for paying the contingency fee of the plaintiff's attorney.

Defendants have however gained some traction with trial courts at this point with arguments that the ACA provides predictable and certain coverage of future medical expenses. Defendants argue that because of the ACA, future health coverage is no longer speculative, since the individual mandate insures medical coverage for most Americans. The courts in these cases assume that the ACA will survive any change in administration or further Supreme Court decisions. Evidence of coverage and out-of-pocket cost limits under the ACA may prove to be useful to defendants seeking to limit future damages, as well as introduction of evidence of the ACA's identified "essential health benefits" that must be covered by most health insurance plans. These benefits include hospitalization, mental health services, prescription drugs, laboratory services, preventive and wellness services and chronic disease management, pediatric services, including oral and vision care, and rehabilitative and habilitative services and devices (such as prosthetics and wheelchairs), as well as physical and occupational therapy.

Two trial court rulings in Ohio are illustrative. In Jones v. MetroHealth Medical Center, No. CV 11-75713 (Cuyahoga County Ohio Court of Common Pleas April 14, 2015), the court ruled, following a post-trial hearing, that an offset of damages was appropriate, in part on the availability of insurance coverage to the plaintiff under the ACA. The court observed as follows: "All of the experts testified that [plaintiff] will qualify for Medicare at age 20 and the plaintiffs' argument that it is possible Medicare will not be available lacks merit. As it exists now, the evidence before the court shows Medicare covers 80 percent of customary and ordinary care. Therefore, the expenses allocated to age 20 for all categories in the Life Care Plan, except Transportation, Home Care and Housing should be set off in their entirety and the amount remaining should then be set off by 80 percent to account for what Medicare would cover, adding in the cost of care under the Affordable Care Act for the eight-year period until [plaintiff] becomes eligible for Medicare and then deducting the previous three years allocated to Transportation. Therefore, after all of the deductions, [plaintiff]'s award for future economic damages should be reduced to $2,951,291 [from $8,000,000]. Additionally, the court stated that, "[a]t most, [plaintiff]'s premium under the ACA would be $8,000 per year, with $6,500 for maximum out-of-pocket expenses. Multiplying those expenses by the amount of years he could at most be ineligible for Medicaid and/or Medicare, his annual maximum totals $116,000."

In Christy v. Humility of Mary Health Partners, No. 2013 CV 01598 (Trumball County Ohio Court of Common Pleas May 4, 2015), the court denied the plaintiff's pretrial motion to preclude the defendant from (1) introducing past medical bills as evidence of amounts previously accepted as payment by certain medical providers (as opposed to full billing rates) and (2) referencing the ACA or Medicaid. The court declared that evidence of the ACA is admissible "as it is the law of the land." The court also found it improper for the plaintiff to introduce "full billed" future medical costs, suggesting that doing so would grossly overstate the plaintiff's damages.

Do you see flaws in this argument? Do the limitations on Medicaid in those states that have not adopted the ACA expansion, or have imposed onerous proof requirements, counter this argument of lifetime benefits? What about the attempts by insurers in some state exchanges to limit their scope of coverage?

CHAPTER 6

LIABILITY OF HEALTH CARE INSTITUTIONS

■ ■ ■

V. TORT LIABILITY OF MANAGED CARE

C. PHYSICIAN INCENTIVE SYSTEMS

Add at page 506, following *Problem: Wanting the "Best"*, **the following new Note:**

NOTE: THE ACA, NEW DELIVERY SYSTEMS, AND LIABILITY RISKS

Managed care plans disappeared from the liability landscape in the 1990s as plans learned that being a "qualified health plan" gave them immunity through ERISA preemption. The Employee Retirement Income Security Act of 1974 (ERISA) preempts either explicitly, or by U.S. Supreme Court interpretation, the vast majority of managed care plans that are employment based and ERISA-qualified. ERISA preemption shields most MCOs from liability stemming from their physicians' errors and omissions as they pursued cost-cutting strategies. It does not shield the rapidly evolving new payment models such as medical homes and accountable care organizations.

As noted above, managed care programs in the 1990s had three relevant features from a liability perspective. While plans have migrated to a less intense management model since the managed care backlash of the 1990s, the liability issues that the courts faced in the early cases may predict litigation over new forms of delivery like Accountable Care Organizations and Medical Homes.

Physician incentives were central to both quality of care and cost management in managed care plans, and the same is true today with Accountable Care Organizations (ACOs) and other new delivery models. MCOs used utilization review techniques, incentives systems, and gatekeepers to control costs. Medicare pay-for-performance, and the regulatory requirement of ACOs, reintroduce a forceful use of utilization management, but within a more highly specified regulatory framework that reduces the discretion of ACOs and other new models.

The ACA has no provisions that directly address agency relationships or corporate negligence, nor does it explicitly alter the existing common law rules relating to vicarious liability and independent contractors. What the ACA does do, however, is create strong pressures—through centers, demonstration projects, and Medicare reimbursement incentives—for providers to integrate and coordinate their delivery of health care for Medicare recipients. The goal is to develop better coordinated systems of care.

In an accountable care organization, a group of primary care physicians, specialists, and other health professionals (or hospitals) agree to accept joint responsibility for the quality and cost of care provided to their patients. If the ACO meets certain targets, its members receive a financial bonus. ACOS strive to improve quality by streamlining and coordinating services from all providers into one, patient-focused plan, and reducing unnecessary and redundant treatment. The goal of an ACO is to keep patients from entering a hospital and cost-effectively treating those that are admitted. ACOs can specifically achieve this goal "by preventing medical errors and eliminating duplication of medical services, including tests, examinations, and other procedures."

ACOs look like mini-health plans and they share some of the design features of the older managed care models. An ACO requires a range of tools to manage patient utilization and to hit quality targets: (1) financial and actuarial tools to establish targets, cost trends, and provider-payment and incentive-distribution models; (2) tools for chronic-disease and complex-ease management and wellness-prevention to control demand and improve quality of care; and (3) utilization tools for reporting preauthorization, hospital utilization review, high-tech radiology management, specialty referral management, and pharmacy management to limit medically unnecessary services.

The ACO indeed resembles a more sophisticated version of the managed care model of the 1990s, with major structural and incentive differences. The ACO form is likely to confront the same concerns from patients that the MCO model generated in the 1990s: fear of cost-cutting, denial of necessary tests and services, and other fears of rationed care. Here is the nub of the liability problem: reducing hospital admissions and reducing tests will in rare cases result in patient harm, and the plaintiffs will argue that the omissions caused their injuries.

MCOs and ACOs however have important differences. Providers can receive bonuses for keeping patients healthy so that hospitalization is not needed. ACOs will have a governing body to represent ACO providers, suppliers, and Medicare beneficiaries; ACOs will create processes to promote evidence-based medicine, promote patient engagement, internally report on quality and cost, and coordinate care. The federal requirements for ACO operation are much more developed than those that regulate MCOs, which were driven by cost containment goals in the 1990s. The incentives are different, the tools more advanced, and the coordination mandates much more extensive. It is not likely that ACOs and other coordinated care models will generate the adverse events and patient anger that managed care did at its peak in the 1990s.

ACOs, unlike MCOs, are not protected by preemption under the Employee Retirement Income Security Act (ERISA), unless the ACOs contract with an ERISA-qualified plans run by a private employer. Patients enrolled in ACOs are not barred from suit, and so a flurry of litigation can be predicted early in the life cycle of ACOs, as they perfect the institutional tools required by their enabling legislation.

ACOs present a range of liability risks, but these are mostly transitional risks as new systems and technologies are chosen and mastered. However, other liability risks are inherent in ACO structure as established by federal law and regulations. Some possible risks include the following.

1. *Solidification of the Standard of Care.* As ACOs and their providers adapt to the new demands mandated by federal law and deliver quality care at a lower cost, patients may be able to claim substandard care. ACOs are premised on evidence-based medicine. In establishing best practices, ACOs must create clinical guidelines, presumably using evidence-based guidelines that are being developed by various federal initiatives. Any guideline selection process risks a claim that the guideline chosen is inappropriate when applied to a particular patient. The use of evidence-based medicine criteria, reporting on quality and cost metrics, and documentation to show the coordination of care will likely create new duties for physicians and therefore for the ACO itself.

2. *Patient Engagement.* The ACO model is built on a concept of patient engagement and "patient-centeredness." ACOs must promote beneficiary engagement, since the ACA ties patient satisfaction to reimbursement, and must meet "patient-centeredness criteria." This patient focus will facilitate patient buy-in and presumably reduce their inclination to sue for adverse events; it also sets a high benchmark for patient engagement and disappointment. It turns the traditional informed consent duty into a more elaborate engagement process.

3. *Cost Control.* Cost-containment goals and incentive-based payments present a theoretical liability exposure. An ACA provision calling for value-based compensation that pays doctors based on positive outcomes rather than patient volume for Medicare and Medicaid patients is set to go into full effect in 2015. Value-based compensation seeks to balance high value care and lower cost. Meaningful quality measures must be developed to ensure the use of evidence-based quality measures. Reducing or eliminating some diagnostic tests, for example, will risk a missed diagnosis on occasion. Such a missed diagnosis of a disease, which delays treatment, is the foundation of a "loss of a chance" claim for patient harms suffered. The defense of cost

reduction may be a hard sell to juries. Incentive-based compensation may risk resurrecting the old HMO liability arguments of undertreatment leading to patient injury. Incentive-based arguments were however rarely if ever successful in suits brought against MCOs, as the courts understand the balance that providers had to strike between cost-containment and quality of care.

4. *Electronic Health Records.* EHRs provide a clear record of care of ACO plan performance, both its failures and successes. They also provide a record of whether care was evidence-based and document compliance. From a lawyer's perspective, standard of care evidence is critical to any malpractice case and the EHRs may provide a gold mine of information, including possible HIPAA violations.

5. *Non-Physician Health Professional Liability.* The expanded role of nurses and physician assistants as part of ACO teams will lead to increased liability risks for those providers and for the ACO as the "employer" of these teams. Coordination of care in an ACO requires that all providers master new skills in moving patients around the network and sharing information across providers. Vicarious liability principles apply for provider errors so long as they are within the scope of employment. An ACO, particularly a hospital-based one, will be liable for the acts of its nurses and physician assistants, since they are likely to be treated as employees and not independent contractors.

6. *Corporate Structure.* An ACO may be found negligent for "failure to uphold the proper standard of care owed its patient." Corporate negligence principles logically apply to integrated organizations that manage care, whether a patient medical home, an ACO, or some other delivery form that the ACA creates. The courts are willing to look beyond the hospital form in deciding whether a health care entity might be liable for corporate negligence, looking at the entity's scope of responsibility for "for arranging and coordinating the total health care of its patients" and whether it takes an "an active role in patients' care".

Institutional liability extends beyond hospitals. A group practice has been held to corporate negligence standards for their lack of a formal on-call backup system in the case of a patient who developed erectile dysfunction after receiving heparin for his post-surgery deep-vein thrombosis (DVT) and had to wait at least 12 hours for treatment for heparin-induced priapism on a holiday weekend. Nursing homes likewise have been included as institutions subject to corporate negligence.

See generally Barry R. Furrow, Medical Malpractice in Perspective, in *Oxford Handbook of American Health Law* (I. Glenn Cohen, Allison Hoffman, and William M. Sage, eds.) New York: Oxford University Press (2015). *See also* Ezekiel J. Emanuel, Why Accountable Care Organizations Are Not 1990s Managed Care Redux, 307 JAMA 2261 (2012); Benjamin Harvey and Glenn Cohen, The Looming Threat of Liability for Accountable Care Organizations and What to Do About It, 310 JAMA 141 (2013).

CHAPTER 7

HEALTH CARE COST AND ACCESS: THE POLICY CONTEXT

■ ■ ■

II. ACCESS AND THE AFFORDABLE CARE ACT

A. INTRODUCTION

Add at page 541 at the end of the current Introduction:

As the Affordable Care Act passes its sixth birthday and the exchanges, now called marketplaces, near their fourth year, the ACA seems a qualified success. Only 9.1 percent of Americans remain uninsured in 2015 according to the National Health Interview Survey, the lowest percentage on record. About 12.7 million individuals were enrolled in coverage through the marketplaces as of the beginning of 2016, with about 85 percent of federally facilitated marketplace enrollees receiving premium tax credits and almost 60 percent receiving cost-sharing reductions. Health care costs have grown at historically low rates in the half decade following the enactment of the ACA, and while, not surprisingly, costs have bumped up some as coverage expanded, cost inflation is well below the levels experienced through the preceding half century.

On the other hand, opinion polls find that the ACA remains more disliked than liked, although many of the dissatisfied would like to see it expanded rather than repealed. Republicans in Congress have tried repeatedly to repeal the legislation, although total repeal is an increasingly a chimerical notion as the ACA has become deeply embedded in our healthcare system. Opponents have filed dozens of lawsuits challenging the ACA or its implementation, largely unsuccessfully.

Although marketplace premiums came in initially at lower than expected levels, they have been climbing steadily as marketplace enrollees have turned out to be older and sicker than insurers had hoped. The standard silver plans have high deductibles and insurers have increasingly turned toward narrower provider networks to hold premiums in check. But surveys show that medical debt problems are decreasing, as is uncompensated care at hospitals, while most consumers are satisfied with marketplace coverage.

A great deal has happened in terms of rules and guidance since the casebook was published in 2013, faithfully chronicled at http://health affairs.org/blog/topics/following-the-aca/. Because Congress has been gridlocked since Republicans took control of the House in 2010, however, there have been few significant amendments to the statute itself. There have been many changes implemented through regulation and guidance, but most changes, other than annual updating of the various program financial thresholds and limits, have been quite technical.

B. PREMIUM ASSISTANCE TAX CREDITS: SECTION 1401

Add at page 543 at the end of section B:

The Supreme Court resolved in 2015 a series of lawsuits claiming that premium tax credits could only be offered through state-based marketplaces.

KING V. BURWELL
Supreme Court of the United States, 2015.
135 S.Ct. 2480.

CHIEF JUSTICE ROBERTS delivered the opinion of the Court.

The Patient Protection and Affordable Care Act adopts a series of interlocking reforms designed to expand coverage in the individual health insurance market. First, the Act bars insurers from taking a person's health into account when deciding whether to sell health insurance or how much to charge. Second, the Act generally requires each person to maintain insurance coverage or make a payment to the Internal Revenue Service. And third, the Act gives tax credits to certain people to make insurance more affordable.

In addition to those reforms, the Act requires the creation of an "Exchange" in each State—basically, a marketplace that allows people to compare and purchase insurance plans. The Act gives each State the opportunity to establish its own Exchange, but provides that the Federal Government will establish the Exchange if the State does not.

This case is about whether the Act's interlocking reforms apply equally in each State no matter who establishes the State's Exchange. Specifically, the question presented is whether the Act's tax credits are available in States that have a Federal Exchange.

The Patient Protection and Affordable Care Act, [ ] grew out of a long history of failed health insurance reform. In the 1990s, several States began experimenting with ways to expand people's access to coverage. One common approach was to impose a pair of insurance market regulations—

a "guaranteed issue" requirement, which barred insurers from denying coverage to any person because of his health, and a "community rating" requirement, which barred insurers from charging a person higher premiums for the same reason. Together, those requirements were designed to ensure that anyone who wanted to buy health insurance could do so.

The guaranteed issue and community rating requirements achieved that goal, but they had an unintended consequence: They encouraged people to wait until they got sick to buy insurance. * * * This consequence— known as "adverse selection"—led to a second: Insurers were forced to increase premiums to account for the fact that, more and more, it was the sick rather than the healthy who were buying insurance. And that consequence fed back into the first: As the cost of insurance rose, even more people waited until they became ill to buy it.

* * *

In 1996, Massachusetts adopted the guaranteed issue and community rating requirements and experienced similar results. But in 2006, Massachusetts added two more reforms: The Commonwealth required individuals to buy insurance or pay a penalty, and it gave tax credits to certain individuals to ensure that they could afford the insurance they were required to buy. [ ] The combination of these three reforms—insurance market regulations, a coverage mandate, and tax credits—reduced the uninsured rate in Massachusetts to 2.6 percent, by far the lowest in the Nation. [ ]

The Affordable Care Act adopts a version of the three key reforms that made the Massachusetts system successful. First, the Act adopts the guaranteed issue and community rating requirements. * * *

Second, the Act generally requires individuals to maintain health insurance coverage or make a payment to the IRS. * * *

Third, the Act seeks to make insurance more affordable by giving refundable tax credits to individuals with household incomes between 100 percent and 400 percent of the federal poverty line. * * *

These three reforms are closely intertwined. As noted, Congress found that the guaranteed issue and community rating requirements would not work without the coverage requirement. [ ] And the coverage requirement would not work without the tax credits. * * *

In addition to those three reforms, the Act requires the creation of an "Exchange" in each State where people can shop for insurance, usually online. [ ] An Exchange may be created in one of two ways. First, the Act provides that "[e]ach State shall . . . establish an American Health Benefit Exchange . . . for the State." [ ] Second, if a State nonetheless chooses not to establish its own Exchange, the Act provides that the Secretary of

Health and Human Services "shall ... establish and operate such Exchange within the State." [ ]

The issue in this case is whether the Act's tax credits are available in States that have a Federal Exchange rather than a State Exchange. The Act initially provides that tax credits "shall be allowed" for any "applicable taxpayer." [ ] The Act then provides that the amount of the tax credit depends in part on whether the taxpayer has enrolled in an insurance plan through "an Exchange established by the State under section 1311 of the Patient Protection and Affordable Care Act [ ]

The IRS addressed the availability of tax credits by promulgating a rule that made them available on both State and Federal Exchanges. * * * At this point, 16 States and the District of Columbia have established their own Exchanges; the other 34 States have elected to have HHS do so.

Petitioners are four individuals who live in Virginia, which has a Federal Exchange. They do not wish to purchase health insurance. In their view, Virginia's Exchange does not qualify as "an Exchange established by the State under [42 U.S.C. § 18031]," so they should not receive any tax credits. That would make the cost of buying insurance more than eight percent of their income, which would exempt them from the Act's coverage requirement. [ ]

Under the IRS Rule, however, Virginia's Exchange would qualify as "an Exchange established by the State under [42 U.S.C. § 18031]," so petitioners would receive tax credits. That would make the cost of buying insurance less than eight percent of petitioners' income, which would subject them to the Act's coverage requirement. The IRS Rule therefore requires petitioners to either buy health insurance they do not want, or make a payment to the IRS.

Petitioners challenged the IRS Rule in Federal District Court. The District Court dismissed the suit, holding that the Act unambiguously made tax credits available to individuals enrolled through a Federal Exchange. [ ] The Court of Appeals for the Fourth Circuit affirmed. The Fourth Circuit viewed the Act as "ambiguous and subject to at least two different interpretations." [ ] The court therefore deferred to the IRS's interpretation. * * *

The Affordable Care Act addresses tax credits in what is now Section 36B of the Internal Revenue Code. That section provides: "In the case of an applicable taxpayer, there shall be allowed as a credit against the tax imposed by this subtitle ... an amount equal to the premium assistance credit amount." [ ] Section 36B then defines the term "premium assistance credit amount" as "the sum of the premium assistance amounts determined under paragraph (2) with respect to all coverage months of the taxpayer occurring during the taxable year." [ ] Section 36B goes on to define the two italicized terms—"premium assistance amount" and "coverage month"—in part by referring to an insurance plan that is enrolled in through "an Exchange established by the State under [42 U.S.C. § 18031]." [ ]

* * *

When analyzing an agency's interpretation of a statute, we often apply the two-step framework announced in Chevron, [ ]. Under that framework, we ask whether the statute is ambiguous and, if so, whether the agency's interpretation is reasonable. [ ] This approach "is premised on the theory that a statute's ambiguity constitutes an implicit delegation from Congress to the agency to fill in the statutory gaps." [ ] "In extraordinary cases, however, there may be reason to hesitate before concluding that Congress has intended such an implicit delegation." [ ]

This is one of those cases. The tax credits are among the Act's key reforms, involving billions of dollars in spending each year and affecting the price of health insurance for millions of people. Whether those credits are available on Federal Exchanges is thus a question of deep "economic and political significance" that is central to this statutory scheme; had Congress wished to assign that question to an agency, it surely would have done so expressly. [ ] It is especially unlikely that Congress would have delegated this decision to the IRS, which has no expertise in crafting health insurance policy of this sort. [ ] This is not a case for the IRS.

It is instead our task to determine the correct reading of Section 36B. If the statutory language is plain, we must enforce it according to its terms. [ ]. But oftentimes the "meaning—or ambiguity—of certain words or phrases may only become evident when placed in context." [ ] So when deciding whether the language is plain, we must read the words "in their context and with a view to their place in the overall statutory scheme." * * *

We begin with the text of Section 36B. As relevant here, Section 36B allows an individual to receive tax credits only if the individual enrolls in an insurance plan through "an Exchange established by the State under [42 U.S.C. § 18031]." In other words, three things must be true: First, the individual must enroll in an insurance plan through "an Exchange." Second, that Exchange must be "established by the State." And third, that Exchange must be established "under [42 U.S.C. § 18031]." We address each requirement in turn.

First, all parties agree that a Federal Exchange qualifies as "an Exchange" for purposes of Section 36B. [ ] Section 18031 provides that "[e]ach State shall . . . establish an American Health Benefit Exchange . . . for the State." [ ] Although phrased as a requirement, the Act gives the States "flexibility" by allowing them to "elect" whether they want to establish an Exchange. § 18041(b). If the State chooses not to do so, Section 18041 provides that the Secretary "shall . . . establish and operate such Exchange within the State." [ ]

By using the phrase "such Exchange," Section 18041 instructs the Secretary to establish and operate the same Exchange that the State was directed to establish under Section 18031. [ ] In other words, State Exchanges and Federal Exchanges are equivalent—they must meet the same requirements, perform the same functions, and serve the same purposes. * * * A Federal Exchange therefore counts as "an Exchange" under Section 36B.

Second, we must determine whether a Federal Exchange is "established by the State" for purposes of Section 36B. At the outset, it might seem that a Federal Exchange cannot fulfill this requirement. * * * But when read in context, "with a view to [its] place in the overall statutory scheme," the meaning of the phrase "established by the State" is not so clear. [ ]

After telling each State to establish an Exchange, Section 18031 provides that all Exchanges "shall make available qualified health plans to qualified individuals." [ ] Section 18032 then defines the term "qualified individual" in part as an individual who "resides in the State that established the Exchange." [ ] And that's a problem: If we give the phrase "the State that established the Exchange" its most natural meaning, there would be no "qualified individuals" on Federal Exchanges. * * * As we just mentioned, the Act requires all Exchanges to "make available qualified health plans to qualified individuals"—something an Exchange could not do if there were no such individuals. [ ] And the Act tells the Exchange, in deciding which health plans to offer, to consider "the interests of qualified individuals . . . in the State or States in which such Exchange operates"— again, something the Exchange could not do if qualified individuals did not exist. § 18031(e)(1)(B). This problem arises repeatedly throughout the Act. [ ]

These provisions suggest that the Act may not always use the phrase "established by the State" in its most natural sense. * * * .

Third, we must determine whether a Federal Exchange is established "under [42 U.S.C. § 18031]." * * *

The Act defines the term "Exchange" to mean "an American Health Benefit Exchange established under section 18031." [ ] If we import that definition into Section 18041, the Act tells the Secretary to "establish and operate such 'American Health Benefit Exchange established under section 18031.'" That suggests that Section 18041 authorizes the Secretary to establish an Exchange under Section 18031, not (or not only) under Section 18041. Otherwise, the Federal Exchange, by definition, would not be an "Exchange" at all. [ ]

This interpretation of "under [42 U.S.C. § 18031]" fits best with the statutory context. All of the requirements that an Exchange must meet are in Section 18031, so it is sensible to regard all Exchanges as established under that provision. In addition, every time the Act uses the word "Exchange," the definitional provision requires that we substitute the phrase "Exchange established under section 18031." If Federal Exchanges were not established under Section 18031, therefore, literally none of the Act's requirements would apply to them. Finally, the Act repeatedly uses the phrase "established under [42 U.S.C. § 18031]" in situations where it would make no sense to distinguish between State and Federal Exchanges. [ ] A Federal Exchange may therefore be considered one established "under [42 U.S.C. § 18031]."

The upshot of all this is that the phrase "an Exchange established by the State under [42 U.S.C. § 18031]" is properly viewed as ambiguous. * * *

* * *

The Affordable Care Act contains more than a few examples of inartful drafting. * * * Anyway, we "must do our best, bearing in mind the fundamental canon of statutory construction that the words of a statute must be read in their context and with a view to their place in the overall statutory scheme." [ ] After reading Section 36B along with other related provisions in the Act, we cannot conclude that the phrase "an Exchange established by the State under [Section 18031]" is unambiguous.

Given that the text is ambiguous, we must turn to the broader structure of the Act to determine the meaning of Section 36B. " * * * Here, the statutory scheme compels us to reject petitioners' interpretation because it would destabilize the individual insurance market in any State with a Federal Exchange, and likely create the very "death spirals" that Congress designed the Act to avoid. [ ]

Under petitioners' reading, * * * the Act would operate quite differently in a State with a Federal Exchange. As they see it, one of the Act's three major reforms—the tax credits—would not apply. And a second major reform—the coverage requirement—would not apply in a meaningful way. As explained earlier, the coverage requirement applies only when the cost of buying health insurance (minus the amount of the tax credits) is less than eight percent of an individual's income. So without the tax credits, the coverage requirement would apply to fewer individuals. And it would be a lot fewer. In 2014, approximately 87 percent of people who bought insurance on a Federal Exchange did so with tax credits, and virtually all of those people would become exempt. [ ] If petitioners are right, therefore, only one of the Act's three major reforms would apply in States with a Federal Exchange.

The combination of no tax credits and an ineffective coverage requirement could well push a State's individual insurance market into a death spiral. * * * And those effects would not be limited to individuals who purchase insurance on the Exchanges. Because the Act requires insurers to treat the entire individual market as a single risk pool, premiums outside the Exchange would rise along with those inside the Exchange. [ ]

It is implausible that Congress meant the Act to operate in this manner. * * *

Petitioners respond that Congress was not worried about the effects of withholding tax credits from States with Federal Exchanges because "Congress evidently believed it was offering states a deal they would not refuse." * * *

Section 18041 refutes the argument that Congress believed it was offering the States a deal they would not refuse. That section provides that, if a State elects not to establish an Exchange, the Secretary "shall . . . establish and operate such Exchange within the State." 42 U.S.C. § 18041(c)(1)(A). The whole point of that provision is to create a federal fallback in case a State chooses not to establish its own Exchange. Contrary to petitioners' argument, Congress did not believe it was offering States a deal they would not refuse—it expressly addressed what would happen if a State did refuse the deal.

Finally, the structure of Section 36B itself suggests that tax credits are not limited to State Exchanges. Section 36B(a) initially provides that tax credits "shall be allowed" for any "applicable taxpayer." Section 36B(c)(1) then defines an "applicable taxpayer" as someone who (among other things) has a household income between 100 percent and 400 percent of the federal poverty line. Together, these two provisions appear to make anyone in the specified income range eligible to receive a tax credit.

According to petitioners, however, those provisions are an empty promise in States with a Federal Exchange. In their view, an applicable taxpayer in such a State would be eligible for a tax credit—but the amount of that tax credit would always be zero. * * *

We have held that Congress "does not alter the fundamental details of a regulatory scheme in vague terms or ancillary provisions." [ ] But in petitioners' view, Congress made the viability of the entire Affordable Care Act turn on the ultimate ancillary provision: a sub-sub-sub section of the Tax Code. We doubt that is what Congress meant to do. * * *

Petitioners' arguments about the plain meaning of Section 36B are strong. But while the meaning of the phrase "an Exchange established by the State under [42 U.S.C. § 18031]" may seem plain "when viewed in isolation," such a reading turns out to be "untenable in light of [the statute] as a whole." * * *

Reliance on context and structure in statutory interpretation is a "subtle business, calling for great wariness lest what professes to be mere rendering becomes creation and attempted interpretation of legislation becomes legislation itself." [ ] For the reasons we have given, however, such reliance is appropriate in this case, and leads us to conclude that Section 36B allows tax credits for insurance purchased on any Exchange created under the Act. Those credits are necessary for the Federal Exchanges to function like their State Exchange counterparts, and to avoid the type of calamitous result that Congress plainly meant to avoid.

In a democracy, the power to make the law rests with those chosen by the people. Our role is more confined—"to say what the law is." [ ] That is easier in some cases than in others. But in every case we must respect the role of the Legislature, and take care not to undo what it has done. A fair reading of legislation demands a fair understanding of the legislative plan.

Congress passed the Affordable Care Act to improve health insurance markets, not to destroy them. If at all possible, we must interpret the Act in a way that is consistent with the former, and avoids the latter. Section 36B can fairly be read consistent with what we see as Congress's plan, and that is the reading we adopt.

The judgment of the United States Court of Appeals for the Fourth Circuit is

Affirmed.

JUSTICE SCALIA, with whom JUSTICE THOMAS and JUSTICE ALITO join, dissenting.

* * *

This case requires us to decide whether someone who buys insurance on an Exchange established by the Secretary gets tax credits. You would think the answer would be obvious—so obvious there would hardly be a need for the Supreme Court to hear a case about it. In order to receive any money under § 36B, an individual must enroll in an insurance plan through an "Exchange established by the State." The Secretary of Health and Human Services is not a State. So an Exchange established by the Secretary is not an Exchange established by the State—which means people who buy health insurance through such an Exchange get no money under § 36B.

Words no longer have meaning if an Exchange that is not established by a State is "established by the State." * * *

I wholeheartedly agree with the Court that sound interpretation requires paying attention to the whole law, not homing in on isolated words or even isolated sections. Context always matters. Let us not forget, however, why context matters: It is a tool for understanding the terms of the law, not an excuse for rewriting them.

* * *

Any effort to understand rather than to rewrite a law must accept and apply the presumption that lawmakers use words in "their natural and ordinary signification." Far from offering the overwhelming evidence of meaning needed to justify the Court's interpretation, other contextual clues undermine it at every turn. To begin with, other parts of the Act sharply distinguish between the establishment of an Exchange by a State and the establishment of an Exchange by the Federal Government. * * *

Reading the rest of the Act also confirms that, as relevant here, there are only two ways to set up an Exchange in a State: establishment by a State and establishment by the Secretary. [ ]. So saying that an Exchange established by the Federal Government is "established by the State" goes beyond giving words bizarre meanings; it leaves the limiting phrase "by the State" with no operative effect at all. * * *

* * *

Faced with overwhelming confirmation that "Exchange established by the State" means what it looks like it means, the Court comes up with argument after feeble argument to support its contrary interpretation. None of its tries comes close to establishing the implausible conclusion that Congress used "by the State" to mean "by the State or not by the State."

* * *

The Court's next bit of interpretive jiggery-pokery involves other parts of the Act that purportedly presuppose the availability of tax credits on both federal and state Exchanges. It is curious that the Court is willing to subordinate the express words of the section that grants tax credits to the mere implications of other provisions with only tangential connections to tax credits. One would think that interpretation would work the other way around. In any event, each of the provisions mentioned by the Court is perfectly consistent with limiting tax credits to state Exchanges. * * *

* * *

For its next defense of the indefensible, the Court turns to the Affordable Care Act's design and purposes. * * * Statutory design and purpose matter only to the extent they help clarify an otherwise ambiguous provision. Could anyone maintain with a straight face that § 36B is unclear? To mention just the highlights, the Court's interpretation clashes with a statutory definition, renders words inoperative in at least seven separate provisions of the Act, overlooks the contrast between provisions that say "Exchange" and those that say "Exchange established by the State," gives the same phrase one meaning for purposes of tax credits but an entirely different meaning for other purposes, and (let us not forget) contradicts the ordinary meaning of the words Congress used. * * *

Having gone wrong in consulting statutory purpose at all, the Court goes wrong again in analyzing it. The purposes of a law must be "collected chiefly from its words," not "from extrinsic circumstances." [ ] Only by concentrating on the law's terms can a judge hope to uncover the scheme of the statute, rather than some other scheme that the judge thinks desirable. Like it or not, the express terms of the Affordable Care Act make only two of the three reforms mentioned by the Court applicable in States that do not establish Exchanges. It is perfectly possible for them to operate independently of tax credits. * * *

* * *

Compounding its errors, the Court forgets that it is no more appropriate to consider one of a statute's purposes in isolation than it is to consider one of its words that way. * * * Most relevant here, the Affordable Care Act displays a congressional preference for state participation in the establishment of Exchanges: Each State gets the first opportunity to set up its Exchange, * * * But setting up and running an Exchange involve significant burdens * * * A State would have much less reason to take on these burdens if its citizens could receive tax credits no matter who establishes its Exchange. * * * So even if making credits available on all Exchanges advances the goal of improving healthcare markets, it frustrates the goal of encouraging state involvement in the implementation of the Act. * * *

Worst of all for the repute of today's decision, the Court's reasoning is largely self-defeating. The Court predicts that making tax credits unavailable in States that do not set up their own Exchanges would cause disastrous economic consequences there. If that is so, however, wouldn't one expect States to react by setting up their own Exchanges? And wouldn't that outcome satisfy two of the Act's goals rather than just one: enabling the Act's reforms to work and promoting state involvement in the Act's implementation? * * *

Perhaps sensing the dismal failure of its efforts to show that "established by the State" means "established by the State or the Federal Government," the Court tries to palm off the pertinent statutory phrase as "inartful drafting." [ ] This Court, however, has no free-floating power "to rescue Congress from its drafting errors." * * *

* * *

The Court's decision reflects the philosophy that judges should endure whatever interpretive distortions it takes in order to correct a supposed flaw in the statutory machinery. That philosophy ignores the American people's decision to give Congress "[a]ll legislative Powers" enumerated in the Constitution. [ ] They made Congress, not this Court, responsible for both making laws and mending them. This Court holds only the judicial power—the power to pronounce the law as Congress has enacted it. We lack the prerogative to repair laws that do not work out in practice, just as the people lack the ability to throw us out of office if they dislike the solutions we concoct. * * *

Trying to make its judge-empowering approach seem respectful of congressional authority, the Court asserts that its decision merely ensures that the Affordable Care Act operates the way Congress "meant [it] to operate." [ ] First of all, what makes the Court so sure that Congress "meant" tax credits to be available everywhere? Our only evidence of what Congress meant comes from the terms of the law, and those terms show beyond all question that tax credits are available only on state Exchanges. More importantly, the Court forgets that ours is a government of laws and not of men. That means we are governed by the terms of our laws, not by the unenacted will of our lawmakers. * * *

* * *

Today's opinion changes the usual rules of statutory interpretation for the sake of the Affordable Care Act. That, alas, is not a novelty. In National Federation of Independent Business v. Sebelius, [ ] this Court revised major components of the statute in order to save them from unconstitutionality. * * * Having transformed two major parts of the law, the Court today has turned its attention to a third. The Act that Congress passed makes tax credits available only on an "Exchange established by the State." This Court, however, concludes that this limitation would prevent the rest of the Act from working as well as hoped. So it rewrites the law to make tax credits available everywhere. We should start calling this law SCOTUScare.

Perhaps the Patient Protection and Affordable Care Act will attain the enduring status of the Social Security Act or the Taft-Hartley Act; perhaps not. But this Court's two decisions on the Act will surely be remembered through the years. The somersaults of statutory interpretation they have performed ("penalty" means tax, "further [Medicaid] payments to the State" means only incremental Medicaid payments to the State, "established by the State" means not established by the State) will be cited by litigants endlessly, to the confusion of honest jurisprudence. And the cases will publish forever the discouraging truth that the Supreme Court of the United States favors some laws over others, and is prepared to do whatever it takes to uphold and assist its favorites.

I dissent.

C. COST–SHARING REDUCTION PAYMENTS: SECTION 1402

Add at page 544 at the end of section C:

In July 30, 2014 the Republican majority in the House of Representatives voted to file a lawsuit challenging the administration's implementation of the Affordable Care Act (ACA). The complaint, filed on November 21, 2014, focused on two issues: the decision by the administration in 2013 to delay the implementation of the employer mandate for a year, and the funding by the administration of the ACA's cost-sharing reduction (CSR) payments without, arguably, an explicit appropriation.

The administration moved to dismiss the House's complaint, relying on well-established precedent in contending that the federal courts have no jurisdiction to hear complaints by members of Congress challenging the actions of the executive. In an order entered on September 9, 2015, Judge Rosemary Collyer of the U.S. District Court for the District of Columbia agreed to dismiss the House's complaint regarding the employer mandate delay issue, which she regarded as a routine dispute over interpretation of the law. (130 F. Supp. 3d 53.)

Judge Collyer refused, however, to dismiss the House's claim that the funding of the CSRs without an explicit annual appropriation infringed on the constitutional authority of Congress to appropriate funds. In October of 2015 Judge Collyer denied the government's request for an expedited appeal from her decision and set the case for briefing on the merits.

On May 12, 2016, Judge Collyer decided (2016 WL 2750934) that the Obama administration could not constitutionally reimburse insurers for the costs they incur in fulfilling their obligation under the ACA to reduce cost sharing for marketplace enrollees with incomes below 250 percent of the poverty level. Judge Collyer found that Congress has not specifically appropriated money for this purpose, and that payments without an appropriation were illegal and unconstitutional.

The judge stayed her order enjoining the administration from reimbursing insurers absent a specific appropriation pending appeal. The administration has appealed the case and it will likely be a long time before it is finally resolved.

If the CSR payments to insurers are stopped, insurers would still remain legally required to reduce cost sharing—at a cost $7 billion this year and $130 billion over the next ten years—without reimbursement. Burdened with this cost without reimbursement, many insurers might cease to offer marketplace coverage. Those that remained would have to raise rates dramatically to cover the costs of reducing cost sharing while ensuring solvency.

Most of this increase would be covered by increased premium tax credits. Indeed, the increased rates might make some individuals eligible for tax credits who might not have been eligible otherwise, resulting in the paradoxical situation in which eliminating appropriations for cost-sharing reduction could increase federal spending, by an estimated $47 billion over ten years. Linda Blumberg and Matthew Buettgens, The Implications of a Finding for the Plaintiffs in House v. Burwell (2016). http://www.urban. org/research/publication/implications-finding-plaintiffs-house-v-burwell.

Higher-income enrollees, on the other hand, could face unsustainable premium increases in the marketplace and would leave the marketplace to find coverage elsewhere. Because individuals would be drawn to the higher tax credits now available through the marketplaces, however, a decision for the House could reduce the number of the uninsured, if the insurers participating in the marketplaces could survive the chaotic transition to higher premiums and tax credits.

Alternatively, insurers would turn to Congress, and possibly to the courts. They could sue in the Court of Claims to be reimbursed by the government for money that they had been promised, but they might also sue claiming that the government could not constitutionally require them to reduce cost sharing without reimbursement. Of course, Congress could simply appropriate funding for the CSRs on an annual basis. But insurers must usually set their premiums for the next year well before Congress appropriates funding. It would be impossible for insurers to set their rates for the coming year not knowing whether there would be an appropriation for the CSRs or not.

H. EMPLOYER RESPONSIBILITY: SECTIONS 1511 THROUGH 1515

Add at page 561 after second paragraph:

The auto-enrollment requirement for large employers was repealed by the Bipartisan Budget Act of 2015.

Add at page 563 before *Problems: Employer Responsibility*:

The high-cost plan (Cadillac plan) excise tax has been delayed until 2020 and may be repealed.

CHAPTER 8

DUTIES TO TREAT

■ ■ ■

II. COMMON LAW APPROACHES

Add at page 591 at the end of *Problem: Ethics and Law: Never the Twain Shall Meet*:

Regulations promulgated by HHS to implement the nondiscrimination requirement of Section 1557 of the ACA (see page 621 of the casebook for the text of the statute) address the application of that requirement to physicians in private practice. Under the statute, physicians in private practice who receive "Federal financial assistance" are prohibited from discriminating in their care of patients on several grounds, including race, sex, age, and disability. According to comments by HHS, the regulations promulgated under Section 1557 will apply to nearly all physicians in practice even though the regulations distinguish among different sources of federal payments. HHS maintains that payments for patient care under Medicare Part B (the program that pays for physician services for Medicare beneficiaries) do not count as "Federal financial assistance" but that payments from Medicaid or other federal programs, including federal payments for adoption of electronic medical record systems that comply with the meaningful use standards will trigger application of Section 1557. (See discussion of HITECH at page 290 of the casebook.) HHS' position on Medicare Part B appears to be contrary to the statute and is likely to be challenged. Nevertheless, physicians in private practice are now prohibited from discriminating. See note below.

III. STATUTORY EXCEPTIONS TO THE COMMON LAW

B. OBLIGATIONS UNDER FEDERAL ANTIDISCRIMINATION STATUTES

Add at page 621 after 42 U.S.C. § 18116:

NOTE ON 42 U.S.C. § 18116 (SECTION 1557 OF THE ACA)

The HHS Office of Civil Rights issued a Final Rule for the implementation of 42 U.S.C. § 18116 (Section 1557 of the ACA) requiring nondiscrimination in health care services that receive federal financial assistance. 81 Fed. Reg. 31376 (May 18, 2016). The Final Rule is described in Section VI.C of Chapter

9 of this supplement. The regulations try to resolve some of the open questions noted in the text. They interpret Section 1557 to reach physicians in private practice (as noted above), for example. The regulations interpret Section 1557 to have created a new right of action specific to health care rather than simply extending the reach of existing federal nondiscrimination statutes. In particular, this allows plaintiffs to bring disparate impact claims without proof of intentional discrimination. Future litigation may address the issue of the appropriate deference to this interpretation of the statute.

A small handful of federal district courts have had the opportunity to interpret and apply Section 1557. Two of these cases disagreed over whether Section 1557 creates a new right of action or merely extends the reach of pre-existing federal nondiscrimination statutes.

In Rumble v. Fairview Health Services, No. 14-CV-2037 SRN/FLN, 2015 WL 1197415 (D. Minn. Mar. 16, 2015), the court, citing Sidney Watson's article cited on page 621 of the casebook, concludes that

> [L]ooking at Section 1557 and the Affordable Care Act as a whole, it appears that Congress intended to create a new, health-specific, anti-discrimination cause of action that is subject to a singular standard, regardless of a plaintiff's protected class status.

The court describes the differing procedures, standards, and burdens plaintiffs would be held to meet if each class needed to comply with the pre-existing federal nondiscrimination statutes. It also notes that these differing standards would be particularly difficult in intersectional claims of discrimination. The court, however, leaves the determination of an appropriate Section 1557 framework for later development. In this case, the court considered plaintiff's claim that the hospital, emergency room, physicians, nurses discriminated against him based on his transgender identity and, therefore, on the basis of sex under the standards used for the relevant federal statutes. The court denied defendants' motion to dismiss plaintiff's claims.

In Southeastern Penn. Transp. Auth. v. Gilead Sciences, 102 F. Supp. 3d 688 (E.D. Pa. 2015), plaintiffs claimed that Gilead's pricing of its Hepatitis C drug resulted in discrimination based on disability and had a disparate impact on minorities. The court held that the reference to the specific federal nondiscrimination statutes both established the protected classes and required that plaintiffs meet the standards and burdens of proof of the specific nondiscrimination statute covering their class and claim. The court dismissed plaintiffs' claim that the pricing discriminated against persons with Hepatitis C commenting that plaintiffs presented a "hodgepodge of complaints about the unfairness of how pharmaceutical companies adjust pricing to accommodate international markets or bulk purchasers" rather than evidence of disability discrimination. For plaintiffs' claim of race discrimination, the court applied the Title VI standard requiring plaintiffs to raise an inference in their pleadings of intentional race discrimination, rather than disparate impact. The court allowed for the plaintiffs to satisfy this standard with evidence of "deliberate indifference" where the defendant knew of the harm to the protected class and fails to act. The court dismissed plaintiffs' race claim for failing to meet these standards. (The "deliberate indifference" approach to proving intentional discrimination has migrated from Title IX litigation in education to Title VI and Rehabilitation Act litigation. (See, e.g., Blunt v. Lower Merion Sch. Dist., 767 F.3d 247 (3d Cir. 2014); Liese v. Indian River County Hosp. District, 701 F.3d 334 (11th Cir. 2012).)

The court in Callum v. CVS Health Corp., 137 F. Supp. 3d 817 (D.S.C. 2015), denied the defendants' motion to dismiss the plaintiff's action for failure to state a claim of race and disability discrimination under Section 1557. Physicians for plaintiff, a veteran of active military service with a diagnosis of PTSD and related disorders including acute agoraphobia, devised a treatment plan to allow him to shop in retail stores without other people around. Several retail stores, including grocery and electronics stores, accommodated this request, but all the CVS stores he contacted denied that accommodation even though corporate stated that the manager had discretion to accommodate him. In addition, plaintiff's pleadings described incidents of behavior by managers that were racially offensive and aggressive, giving rise to his claim of race discrimination. The court held that CVS, a retail pharmacy providing prescribed medications, was a "health program or activity" and a covered entity under Section 1557, relying in part on proposed regulations issued by HHS at that time. In addition, the court held that CVS received "federal financial assistance" in the form of Medicare and Medicaid payment for prescribed medications.

CHAPTER 9

PRIVATE HEALTH INSURANCE AND MANAGED CARE: LIABILITY AND STATE AND FEDERAL REGULATION

■ ■ ■

VI. INSURANCE REGULATION UNDER THE AFFORDABLE CARE ACT

A. UNDERWRITING REFORMS

Add at page 670 at the end of Note 3:

The Americans with Disabilities Act (ADA) generally prohibits employers with 15 or more employees from obtaining medical information from employees through disability-related inquiries or medical examinations. It does, however, allow employers to make medical inquiries or conduct medical examinations as part of a "voluntary" employee health program, which includes workplace wellness programs.

The Genetic Information Nondiscrimination Act (GINA) prohibits employers with 15 or more employees from requesting, requiring, or purchasing genetic information regarding their employees unless one or more of six narrow exceptions applies. Genetic information includes information about the "manifestations of a disease or disorder in family members of an individual." Family members obviously include spouses and children.

One of the exceptions to GINA's information request prohibitions applies when an employee voluntarily accepts health services from the employer, which can include wellness program services. The question thus arises under both the ADA and GINA as to when wellness programs may legally offer incentives to obtain "voluntarily" current or past health information regarding employees or the spouses or children of employees.

In May of 2016 the Equal Employment Opportunities Commission released final regulations delineating when collection of health information on employees and their family members was permissible under the ADA and GINA, see Timothy Jost, EEOC Rules Allow Significant Rewards and Penalties in Connection with Wellness Program Participation, http://healthaffairs.org/blog/2016/05/17/eeoc-rules-allow-significant-rewards-penalties-in-connection-with-wellness-program-participation/.

The EEOC regulations largely track the requirements imposed by the ACA and tri-department regulations promulgated under it described in the casebook, although they apply to all employer-sponsored workplace wellness programs and not just those associated with employer-sponsored health plans. Employers may only offer incentives or impose penalties for the collection of information from employees or their spouses if the wellness program is reasonably designed to promote health, incentives or penalties do not exceed 30 percent of the cost of sole employee coverage (plus an additional 30 percent if medical information on spouses is requested), and confidentiality of medical information must be protected. The GINA regulations do not permit employers to offer incentives or impose penalties for the provision of medical information on children.

B. MINIMUM ESSENTIAL BENEFIT AND COST–SHARING REQUIREMENTS

1. Requirements Effective in 2014: Section 1302

Add at page 672 after first full paragraph:

The Protecting Affordable Coverage for Employees (PACE) act, enacted in October of 2015, allowed states to choose a "small group employer" definition of either 2–50 employees or 2–100 employees. Most states have chosen to retain the traditional 2–50 definition, although a few have expanded to 100.

Add at page 674 after run-over paragraph:

A 2014 amendment to the ACA removed the prohibition against small group plans imposing deductibles that exceeded $2000 for individuals or $4000 for families.

Add at page 677 at end of Note 2:

For a discussion of the ongoing litigation involving religious freedom challenges to the contraceptive coverage requirement imposed by the preventive services mandate, see chapter 15.

C. INSURANCE REFORMS: SECTIONS 1001, 1003, 10101

Add at page 680 at end of note on Discrimination:

Section 1557 of the ACA provides that an individual shall not, on the basis of race, color, national origin, sex, age, or disability, be "excluded from participation in, denied the benefits of, or subjected to discrimination under any health program or activity of which any part receives federal financial assistance, or any program or activity that is administered by an agency of the federal government or any entity established under Title I of the ACA (the private insurance reform and affordability title)."

The HHS Office of Civil Rights finalized rules implementing section 1557 in May of 2016. The rules are lengthy and comprehensive. They define federal financial assistance to include grants, loans, credits, subsidies, and insurance contracts. Under this definition, health insurers that receive premium tax credits or cost-sharing reduction payments for enrollees receive federal financial assistance, but providers that they pay in turn do not thereby receive assistance (although most of these providers probably receive federal assistance in other forms, such as Medicare or Medicaid). The rule does not apply to physicians who participate only in Medicare Part B, although it does cover all physicians who receive Medicaid or meaningful use information technology (IT) funding (which ends in 2018). Most doctors are covered.

The final rule requires covered entities to post nondiscrimination notices and to include nondiscrimination notices in significant publications and communications. The rule prohibits discrimination against individuals with limited English proficiency. It requires language assistance generally and in particular the availability of qualified interpreters. The final regulations also require effective communications with individuals with disabilities, including the provision of auxiliary aids and services to individuals with impaired sensory, manual, or speaking skills.

Section 1557 further prohibits discrimination on the basis of sex. Sex discrimination is defined by the final rule to include discrimination on the basis of pregnancy, false pregnancy, termination of pregnancy or recovery from it, childbirth, or sex stereotyping (including the stereotype that an individual must identify as either male or female). The final rule prohibits discrimination based on gender identity, which may be different from the sex assigned to an individual at birth. Gender identity is defined in the final rule to include identity as "male, female, neither, or a combination of male and female." Covered entities must treat transgender individuals consistently with their own gender identity.

The final rule does not resolve whether sexual orientation (sexual preference) discrimination is as such a form of sex discrimination prohibited by 1557. It rather states that OCR will evaluate complaints based on sexual orientation to determine whether they involve discriminatory stereotyping of sexual attraction or behavior. The preamble states that HHS supports prohibiting sexual orientation discrimination as a policy matter and will continue to monitor legal developments. It also notes that sexual orientation discrimination by health insurance marketplaces and insurers offering qualified health plans is already prohibited.

The proposed rule left open the question of whether the rule should recognize exceptions to the discrimination rule, for example based on religious belief. The final rule provides that where application of any requirement of the rule would violate applicable Federal statutes protecting religious freedom and conscience, that application will not be required. These would include, for example, the Religious Freedom Restoration Act, the provisions of the ACA related to abortion services, and the regulations issued under the ACA with respect to preventive services.

Individuals may sue directly under section 1557 in federal court. HHS has concluded that section 1557 provides a new, health-specific, anti-discrimination cause of action subject to a single standard, regardless of the plaintiff's protected class status. The preamble concludes, therefore, that an individual can bring a private action based on disparate impact discrimination even though a disparate impact claim would not be available for the specific form of discrimination under the underlying statutory prohibition. The final rule also clarifies that compensatory damages are available in 1557 actions. Attorneys' fee and class action rules that apply under the underlying statutes also apply to 1557 claims.

Add at page 684 at end of Note 2:

As of 2014, student health programs may no longer impose annual limits on essential health benefits. Student health plans are not required to offer health plans keyed to specific metal levels, but cannot offer plans that have actuarial values of less than 60 percent.

VII. THE EMPLOYEE RETIREMENT INCOME SECURITY ACT OF 1974: ERISA

A. ERISA PREEMPTION OF STATE HEALTH INSURANCE REGULATION

Add at page 697 in addition to or in place of *Rush v. Moran*:

Litigation concerning ERISA's preemption provisions continues, with the latest Supreme Court decision concerning all-payer claims databases.

GOBEILLE V. LIBERTY MUTUAL INSURANCE COMPANY
Supreme Court of the United States, 2016.
136 S.Ct. 936.

JUSTICE KENNEDY delivered the opinion of the Court.

This case presents a challenge to the applicability of a state law requiring disclosure of payments relating to health care claims and other information relating to health care services. Vermont enacted the statute so it could maintain an all-inclusive health care database. [ ] The state law, by its terms, applies to health plans established by employers and regulated by the Employee Retirement Income Security Act of 1974

(ERISA), [ ] The question before the Court is whether ERISA pre-empts the Vermont statute as it applies to ERISA plans.

Vermont requires certain public and private entities that provide and pay for health care services to report information to a state agency. The reported information is compiled into a database reflecting "all health care utilization, costs, and resources in [Vermont], and health care utilization and costs for services provided to Vermont residents in another state." [ ] A database of this kind is sometimes called an all-payer claims database, for it requires submission of data from all health insurers and other entities that pay for health care services. Almost 20 States have or are implementing similar databases. [ ]

Vermont's law requires health insurers, health care providers, health care facilities, and governmental agencies to report any "information relating to health care costs, prices, quality, utilization, or resources required" by the state agency, including data relating to health insurance claims and enrollment. [ ] Health insurers must submit claims data on members, subscribers, and policyholders. [ ] The Vermont law defines health insurer to include a "self-insured . . . health care benefit plan," [ ] as well as "any third party administrator" and any "similar entity with claims data, eligibility data, provider files, and other information relating to health care provided to a Vermont resident." [ ] The database must be made "available as a resource for insurers, employers, providers, purchasers of health care, and State agencies to continuously review health care utilization, expenditures, and performance in Vermont." [ ]

Vermont law leaves to a state agency the responsibility to "establish the types of information to be filed under this section, and the time and place and the manner in which such information shall be filed." [ ] The law has been implemented by a regulation creating the Vermont Healthcare Claims Uniform Reporting and Evaluation System. The regulation requires the submission of "medical claims data, pharmacy claims data, member eligibility data, provider data, and other information," [ ] in accordance with specific formatting, coding, and other requirements [ ] Under the regulation, health insurers must report data about the health care services provided to Vermonters regardless of whether they are treated in Vermont or out-of-state and about non-Vermonters who are treated in Vermont. * * *

Covered entities (reporters) must register with the State and must submit data monthly, quarterly, or annually, depending on the number of individuals that an entity serves. * * * Entities with fewer than 200 members need not report at all, [ ], and are termed "voluntary" reporters as distinct from "mandated" reporters, [ ] Reporters can be fined for not complying with the statute or the regulation. [ ]

Respondent Liberty Mutual Insurance Company maintains a health plan (Plan) that provides benefits in all 50 States to over 80,000 individuals, comprising respondent's employees, their families, and former employees. The Plan is self-insured and self-funded, which means that Plan benefits are paid by respondent. The Plan, which qualifies as an "employee welfare benefit plan" under ERISA, [ ], is subject to "ERISA's comprehensive regulation," [ ] Respondent, as the Plan sponsor, is both a fiduciary and plan administrator. The Plan uses Blue Cross Blue Shield of Massachusetts, Inc. (Blue Cross) as a third-party administrator. Blue Cross manages the "processing, review, and payment" of claims for respondent. * * * The Plan is a voluntary reporter under the Vermont regulation because it covers some 137 Vermonters, which is fewer than the 200-person cutoff for mandated reporting. Blue Cross, however, serves several thousand Vermonters, and so it is a mandated reporter. Blue Cross, therefore, must report the information it possesses about the Plan's members in Vermont.

In August 2011, Vermont issued a subpoena ordering Blue Cross to transmit to a state-appointed contractor all the files it possessed on member eligibility, medical claims, and pharmacy claims for Vermont members. * * * The penalty for noncompliance, Vermont threatened, would be a fine of up to $2,000 a day and a suspension of Blue Cross' authorization to operate in Vermont for as long as six months. [ ] Respondent, concerned in part that the disclosure of confidential information regarding its members might violate its fiduciary duties under the Plan, instructed Blue Cross not to comply. Respondent then filed this action in the United States District Court for the District of Vermont. It sought a declaration that ERISA pre-empts application of Vermont's statute and regulation to the Plan and an injunction forbidding Vermont from trying to acquire data about the Plan or its members.

* * * The District Court granted summary judgment to Vermont. * * *

The Court of Appeals for the Second Circuit reversed. * * *

The text of ERISA's express pre-emption clause is the necessary starting point. It is terse but comprehensive. ERISA pre-empts "any and all State laws insofar as they may now or hereafter relate to any employee benefit plan." 29 U.S.C. § 1144(a).

The Court has addressed the potential reach of this clause before. In Travelers, the Court observed that "[i]f 'relate to' were taken to extend to the furthest stretch of its indeterminacy, then for all practical purposes pre-emption would never run its course." [ ] That is a result "no sensible person could have intended." [ ] So the need for workable standards has led the Court to reject "uncritical literalism" in applying the clause. [ ]

Implementing these principles, the Court's case law to date has described two categories of state laws that ERISA pre-empts. First, ERISA pre-empts a state law if it has a "'reference to'" ERISA plans. [ ] To be more precise, "[w]here a State's law acts immediately and exclusively upon ERISA plans . . . or where the existence of ERISA plans is essential to the law's operation . . . , that 'reference' will result in pre-emption." [ ] Second, ERISA pre-empts a state law that has an impermissible "connection with" ERISA plans, meaning a state law that "governs . . . a central matter of plan administration" or "interferes with nationally uniform plan administration." [ ] A state law also might have an impermissible connection with ERISA plans if "acute, albeit indirect, economic effects" of the state law "force an ERISA plan to adopt a certain scheme of substantive coverage or effectively restrict its choice of insurers." [ ] When considered together, these formulations ensure that ERISA's express pre-emption clause receives the broad scope Congress intended while avoiding the clause's susceptibility to limitless application.

Respondent contends that Vermont's law falls in the second category of state laws that are pre-empted by ERISA: laws that govern, or interfere with the uniformity of, plan administration and so have an impermissible "'connection with'" ERISA plans. [ ] When presented with these contentions in earlier cases, the Court has considered "the objectives of the ERISA statute as a guide to the scope of the state law that Congress understood would survive," ibid., and "the nature of the effect of the state law on ERISA plans," [ ] Here, those considerations lead the Court to conclude that Vermont's regime, as applied to ERISA plans, is pre-empted.

ERISA does not guarantee substantive benefits. The statute, instead, seeks to make the benefits promised by an employer more secure by mandating certain oversight systems and other standard procedures. [ ] Those systems and procedures are intended to be uniform. [ ] "Requiring ERISA administrators to master the relevant laws of 50 States and to contend with litigation would undermine the congressional goal of 'minimiz[ing] the administrative and financial burden[s]' on plan administrators—burdens ultimately borne by the beneficiaries." [ ]

ERISA's reporting, disclosure, and recordkeeping requirements for welfare benefit plans are extensive. ERISA plans must present participants with a plan description explaining, among other things, the plan's eligibility requirements and claims-processing procedures. [ ] Plans must notify participants when a claim is denied and state the basis for the denial. [ ] Most important for the pre-emption question presented here, welfare benefit plans governed by ERISA must file an annual report with the Secretary of Labor. The report must include a financial statement listing assets and liabilities for the previous year and, further, receipts and disbursements of funds. [ ] * * * Because welfare benefit plans are in the business of providing benefits to plan participants, a plan's reporting of data on disbursements by definition incorporates paid claims. [ ]

The Secretary of Labor has authority to establish additional reporting and disclosure requirements for ERISA plans. ERISA permits the Secretary to use the data disclosed by plans "for statistical and research purposes, and [to] compile and publish such studies, analyses, reports, and surveys based thereon as he may deem appropriate." [ ] The Secretary also may, "in connection" with any research, "collect, compile, analyze, and publish data, information, and statistics relating to" plans. [ ] [The court discusses further ERISA reporting and recordkeeping requirements.]

* * *

Vermont's reporting regime, which compels plans to report detailed information about claims and plan members, both intrudes upon "a central matter of plan administration" and "interferes with nationally uniform plan administration." [ ] The State's law and regulation govern plan reporting, disclosure, and—by necessary implication—recordkeeping. These matters are fundamental components of ERISA's regulation of plan administration. Differing, or even parallel, regulations from multiple jurisdictions could create wasteful administrative costs and threaten to subject plans to wide-ranging liability. [ ] Pre-emption is necessary to prevent the States from imposing novel, inconsistent, and burdensome reporting requirements on plans.

The Secretary of Labor, not the States, is authorized to administer the reporting requirements of plans governed by ERISA. He may exempt plans from ERISA reporting requirements altogether. [ ] And, he may be authorized to require ERISA plans to report data similar to that which Vermont seeks, though that question is not presented here. Either way, the uniform rule design of ERISA makes it clear that these decisions are for federal authorities, not for the separate States.

Vermont disputes the pre-emption of its reporting regime on several fronts. The State argues that respondent has not demonstrated that the reporting regime in fact has caused it to suffer economic costs. [ ] But respondent's challenge is not based on the theory that the State's law must be pre-empted solely because of economic burdens caused by the state law. [ ] Respondent argues, rather, that Vermont's scheme regulates a central aspect of plan administration and, if the scheme is not pre-empted, plans will face the possibility of a body of disuniform state reporting laws and, even if uniform, the necessity to accommodate multiple governmental agencies. A plan need not wait to bring a pre-emption claim until confronted with numerous inconsistent obligations and encumbered with any ensuing costs. Vermont contends, furthermore, that ERISA does not pre-empt the state statute and regulation because the state reporting scheme has different objectives. This Court has recognized that "[t]he principal object of [ERISA] is to protect plan participants and beneficiaries." [ ] And "[i]n enacting ERISA, Congress' primary concern was with the mismanagement of funds accumulated to finance employee benefits and the failure to pay employees benefits from accumulated funds." [ ] The State maintains that its program has nothing to do with the financial solvency of plans or the prudent behavior of fiduciaries. [ ] This does not suffice to avoid federal pre-emption. "[P]re-emption claims turn on Congress's intent." [ ] The purpose of a state law, then, is relevant only as it may relate to the "scope of the state law that Congress understood would survive," [ ] or "the nature of the effect of the state law on ERISA plans," * * * Vermont orders health insurers, including ERISA plans, to report detailed information about the administration of benefits in a systematic manner. This is a direct regulation of a fundamental ERISA function. Any difference in purpose does not transform this direct regulation of "a central matter of plan administration," [ ] into an innocuous and peripheral set of additional rules.

The Vermont regime cannot be saved by invoking the State's traditional power to regulate in the area of public health. The Court in the past has "addressed claims of pre-emption with the starting presumption that Congress does not intend to supplant state law," in particular state laws regulating a subject of traditional state power. [ ] ERISA, however, "certainly contemplated the pre-emption of substantial areas of traditional state regulation." [ ] ERISA pre-empts a state law that regulates a key facet of plan administration even if the state law exercises a traditional state power. [ ] The fact that reporting is a principal and essential feature of ERISA demonstrates that Congress intended to pre-empt state reporting laws like Vermont's, including those that operate with the purpose of furthering public health. The analysis may be different when applied to a state law, such as a tax on hospitals, [ ] the enforcement of which necessitates incidental reporting by ERISA plans; but that is not the law before the Court. Any presumption against pre-emption, whatever its force in other instances, cannot validate a state law that enters a fundamental area of ERISA regulation and thereby counters the federal purpose in the way this state law does.

Respondent suggests that the Patient Protection and Affordable Care Act (ACA), which created new reporting obligations for employer-sponsored health plans and incorporated those requirements into the body of ERISA, further demonstrates that ERISA pre-empts Vermont's reporting regime. [ ] The ACA, however, specified that it shall not "be construed to preempt any State law that does not prevent the application of the provisions" of the ACA. [ ] This anti-pre-emption provision might prevent any new ACA-created reporting obligations from pre-empting state reporting regimes like Vermont's, notwithstanding the incorporation of these requirements in the heart of ERISA. [ ]

The Court has no need to resolve this issue. ERISA's pre-existing reporting, disclosure, and recordkeeping provisions—upon which the

Court's conclusion rests—maintain their pre-emptive force whether or not the new ACA reporting obligations also pre-empt state law.

* * *

Affirmed.

JUSTICE THOMAS, concurring.

I join the Court's opinion because it faithfully applies our precedents interpreting, the express pre-emption provision of the Employee Retirement Income Security Act of 1974 (ERISA). I write separately because I have come to doubt whether § 1144 is a valid exercise of congressional power and whether our approach to ERISA pre-emption is consistent with our broader pre-emption jurisprudence.

Section 1144 contains what may be the most expansive express pre-emption provision in any federal statute. * * * .

Read according to its plain terms, § 1144 raises constitutional concerns. "[T]he Supremacy Clause gives 'supreme' status only to those [federal laws] that are 'made in Pursuance'" of the Constitution. [ ] But I question whether any provision of Article I authorizes Congress to prohibit States from applying a host of generally applicable civil laws to ERISA plans. "The Constitution requires a distinction between what is truly national and what is truly local." [ ] If the Federal Government were "to take over the regulation of entire areas of traditional state concern," including "areas having nothing to do with the regulation of commercial activities," then "the boundaries between the spheres of federal and state authority would blur and political responsibility would become illusory." [ ] Just because Congress can regulate some aspects of ERISA plans pursuant to the Commerce Clause does not mean that Congress can exempt ERISA plans from state regulations that have nothing to do with interstate commerce. [ ]

This Court used to interpret § 1144 according to its text. But we became uncomfortable with how much state law § 1144 would pre-empt if read literally. "If 'relate to' were taken to extend to the furthest stretch of its indeterminacy," we explained, "then for all practical purposes pre-emption would never run its course." * * * Rather than addressing the constitutionality of § 1144, we abandoned efforts to give its text its ordinary meaning. In Travelers, we adopted atextual but what we thought to be "workable" standards to construe § 1144. [ ] Thus, to determine whether a state law impermissibly "relates to" an ERISA plan due to some "connection with" that plan, we now "look both to the objectives of the ERISA statute . . . as well as to the nature of the effect of the state law on ERISA plans." [ ]

We decided Travelers in 1995. I joined that opinion and have joined others applying the approach we adopted in Travelers. But our interpretation of ERISA's express pre-emption provision has become increasingly difficult to reconcile with our pre-emption jurisprudence. * * * Until we confront whether Congress had the constitutional authority to pre-empt such a wide array of state laws in the first place, the Court—and lower courts—will continue to struggle to apply § 1144. It behooves us to address whether Article I gives Congress such power and whether § 1144 may permissibly be read to avoid unconstitutional results.

JUSTICE BREYER, concurring.

I write separately to emphasize that a failure to find pre-emption here would subject self-insured health plans under the Employee Retirement Income Security Act of 1974 [ ] to 50 or more potentially conflicting information reporting requirements. Doing so is likely to create serious administrative problems. * * *

I would also emphasize that pre-emption does not necessarily prevent Vermont or other States from obtaining the self-insured, ERISA-based health-plan information that they need. States wishing to obtain information can ask the Federal Government for appropriate approval. As the majority points out, the "Secretary of Labor has authority to establish additional reporting and disclosure requirements for ERISA plans." [ ] Moreover, the Secretary "is authorized to undertake research and surveys and in connection therewith to collect, compile, analyze and publish data, information, and statistics relating to employee benefit plans, including retirement, deferred compensation, and welfare plans." * * *

I see no reason why the Secretary of Labor could not develop reporting requirements that satisfy the States' needs, including some State-specific requirements, as appropriate. Nor do I see why the Department could not delegate to a particular State the authority to obtain data related to that State, while also providing the data to the Federal Secretary for use by other States or at the federal level.

* * *

For these reasons, and others that the majority sets forth, I agree that Vermont's statute is pre-empted because it "interferes with nationally uniform plan administration." [ ]

JUSTICE GINSBURG, with whom JUSTICE SOTOMAYOR joins, dissenting.

* * *

The majority finds that the burden imposed by the Vermont reporting requirement warrants preemption of the [data-collection] statute. This conclusion falters for two primary reasons. First, the reporting requirement imposed by the Vermont statute differs in kind from the 'reporting' that is required by ERISA and therefore was not the kind of state law Congress intended to preempt. Second, Liberty Mutual has failed to show any actual burden, much less a burden that triggers ERISA preemption. Rather, the Vermont statute . . . does not interfere with an ERISA plan's administration of benefits." [ ]

* * *

To determine whether Vermont's data-collection law, as applied to Liberty's plan, has an impermissible "connection with" ERISA plans, I look first to the "objectives of the ERISA statute as a guide." * * *

Beyond debate, Vermont's data-collection law does not seek to regulate the management and solvency of ERISA-covered welfare plans. * * * Nor does Vermont's statute even arguably regulate relationships among the prime ERISA entities: beneficiaries, participants, administrators, employees, trustees and other fiduciaries, and the plan itself.

Despite these significant differences between ERISA's reporting requirements and Vermont's data-collection regime, Liberty contends that Congress intended to spare ERISA plans from benefit-related reporting requirements unless those requirements are nationally uniform. * * *

* * *

Satisfied that ERISA's objectives do not require preemption of Vermont's data-collection law, I turn to the "nature of the effect of the state law on ERISA plans." [ ] The imposition of some burdens on the administration of ERISA plans, the Court has held, does not suffice to require preemption. * * * Moreover, no "central matter of plan administration," [ ] is touched by Vermont's data-collection law. That law prescribes no vesting requirements, benefit levels, beneficiary designations, or rules on how claims should be processed or paid. Indeed, Vermont's law does not require Liberty to do anything. The burden of compliance falls on Blue Cross, which apparently provides the data without protest on behalf of other self-funded plans. [ ] Reporting and disclosure are no doubt required of ERISA plans, but those requirements are ancillary to the areas ERISA governs. Reporting and recordkeeping incident to state laws of general applicability have been upheld as they bear on ERISA plans. * * *

* * *

The Vermont data-collection statute * * * is generally applicable and does not involve "a central matter of plan administration." [ ] And, as Judge Straub emphasized in his dissent, Liberty "failed to provide any details or showing of the alleged burden," instead "arguing only that 'all regulations have their costs.' " * * * The Court of Appeals majority accentuated the sheer number of data entries that must be reported to Vermont. [ ] Entirely overlooked in that enumeration is the technological capacity for efficient computer-based data storage, formatting, and submission. [ ] Where regulatory compliance depends upon the use of evolving technologies, it should be incumbent on the objector to show concretely what the alleged regulatory burden in fact entails.

Because data-collection laws like Vermont's are not uniform from State to State, compliance is inevitably burdensome, Liberty successfully argued in the Court of Appeals. The Court replays this reasoning in today's opinion. [ ] But state-law diversity is a hallmark of our political system and has been lauded in this Court's opinions. [ ] Something more than an inherent characteristic of our federal system, therefore, must underpin the ERISA-grounded preemption Liberty urges.

* * *

The Court [has taken] care, however, to confine [pre-emption] to issues implicating "a central matter of plan administration," in other words, "a core ERISA concern." [ ] What does that category comprise? As earlier described, [ ] prescriptions on benefit levels, beneficiary designations, vesting requirements, and rules on processing and payment of claims would rank under the central or core ERISA subject-matter rubric. So, too, would reporting and disclosure obligations, * * * that further regulation of the design and administration of employee benefit plans, i.e., reporting and disclosures tied to the areas ERISA governs. * * * Vermont's data-collection law, eliciting information on medical claims, services provided to beneficiaries, charges and payment for those services, and demographic makeup of those receiving benefits, does not fit the bill any more than reporting relating to a plan's taxes or wage payments does.

Numerous States have informed the Court of their urgent need for information yielded by their health care data-collection laws. * * * Wait until the Federal Government acts is the Court's response. * * * It is unsettling, however, to leave the States dependent on a federal agency's grace, i.e., the Department of Labor's willingness to take on a chore divorced from ERISA's objectives.

Declaring "reporting" unmodified, a central or core ERISA function as the Second Circuit did [ ] passes the line this Court drew in Travelers, De Buono, and Dillingham when it reined in § 1144(a) so that it would no longer operate as a "super-preemption" provision. [ ] I dissent from the Court's retrieval of preemption doctrine that belongs in the discard bin.

CHAPTER 10

PUBLIC HEALTH CARE FINANCING PROGRAMS: MEDICARE AND MEDICAID

■ ■ ■

II. MEDICARE

C. PAYMENT FOR SERVICES

3. Medicare Payment of Physicians (Part B)

Add at page 791 at end of first full paragraph:

New Physician Payment Rules for Medicare Under MACRA

On April 16, 2015, Congress passed and President Obama signed into law the Medicare Access and CHIP Reauthorization Act of 2015 (MACRA). MACRA permanently repeals the Sustainable Growth Rate provisions discussed in the text at p. 790 and sunsets the payment adjustments associated with the Physician Quality Reporting System, the Value-Based Payment Modifier, and the Medicare Electronic Health Record (EHR) incentive program, discussed at pages 798 and 1135. Most important, however, are major changes in physician payment under Medicare. Adopted with strong bi-partisan support, the new payment framework is designed to incorporate value-based criteria for fee-for-service payments and speed up adoption of value-based payment models. It does so by establishing a Quality Payment Program that includes two alternative paths for physicians to choose between: the Merit-Based Incentive Payment System (MIPS) and participation in certain Alternative Payment Models (APMs). Beginning in 2017, most physicians will be required to choose whether to be evaluated under MIPS or to participate in an APM; payment adjustments will begin in 2019.

Path 1: MIPS. MIPS combines payment adjustments associated with the sunsetted programs mentioned above into a single consolidated program using four weighted performance categories upon which "eligible clinicians" (which includes physicians, physician assistants, nurse practitioners, clinical nurse specialists, certified registered nurse anesthetists, and groups that include such clinicians) will be assessed. The categories are: Quality; Resource Use; Clinical Practice Improvement Activities; and Meaningful Use of Certified EHR Technology (referred to as Advancing Care Information in the proposed rule). Certain practitioners are exempted, including those that have a low volume of Medicare patients and special exceptions are proposed for "non-patient facing practitioners" (such as those in specialties such as anesthesiology, diagnostic radiology, nuclear medicine, and pathology).

MIPS requires the Secretary of HHS to develop and provide clinicians with a Composite Performance Score that incorporates MIPS performance on each of these categories. Based on this Composite Performance Score, eligible professionals (EPs) may receive an upward, downward, or no payment adjustment. In the first year, depending on the variation of MIPS scores, adjustments are calculated so that negative adjustments can be no more than 4 percent, and positive adjustments are generally up to 4 percent, with additional bonuses for the highest performers. Notably, MACRA requires MIPS to be budget neutral. Therefore, clinicians' positive and negative MIPS scores will approximately cancel each other out. CMS estimates MIPS would award approximately $833 million in positive adjustments and extract $833 million in negative adjustments. However, the agency also estimates that it may pay as much as $500 million in "exceptional performance payments" to clinicians whose performance exceeds a specified threshold. Under the proposed rule, the first performance year for measurement is 2017 which would be used for payment adjustments in 2019.

MIPS requires the Secretary to develop and provide clinicians with a Composite Performance Score that incorporates MIPS EP performance on each of the categories. Clinicians will be able to choose certain measures within each of the following performance categories:

- *Quality* (50 percent of total score in year one): Clinicians would choose six measures from a range of options that accommodate differences among specialties and practices.

- *Advancing Care Information* (25 percent of total score in year one): Clinicians would choose to report customizable measures that reflect how they use technology in their day-to-day practice, with particular emphasis on interoperability and information exchange. (In contrast to the Meaningful Use program which this category replaces, it would not require all or nothing EHR measurement.)

- *Clinical Practice Improvement Activities* (15 percent of total score in year one): Clinicians would be rewarded for improvement activities (e.g., care coordination, beneficiary engagement, and patient safety) which they can choose from a list of 90 possible options that match the clinician's practice goals.

- *Cost* (10 percent of total score in year one): The score is based on Medicare claims using 40 episode-specific measures to account for differences among specialties.

Path 2: Advanced Alternate Payment Models (APMs). In order to encourage physicians to move away from fee-for-service payments that do not reward value, the MACRA offers incentives to accept evolving payment models. Clinicians participating to a sufficient extent in "Advanced APMs" would be exempt from MIPS reporting requirements and would qualify for a five percent Medicare Part B incentive payment. Under the proposed rule, to be an Advanced APM, the model generally must require participants to bear a certain amount of financial risk; base payments on quality measures comparable to those used in the MIPS quality performance category; and require participants to use certified EHR technology. Under the proposed rule, models that would qualify as Advanced APMs include Tracks 2 and 3 of the Medicare Shared Savings Program, Next Generation ACO Model, and Comprehensive Primary Care Plus model. (These programs are discussed at pp. 802–10 of the text.) That Track 1 ACOs (which currently constitute over 95 percent of Medicare ACOs) are not included evidences another effort of CMS to nudge physicians along the path to accepting greater risk. A perhaps unintended consequence may be to add further incentives for physicians to become employed by health systems.

MACRA also takes aim at improving incentives for clinicians who may have heretofore been reluctant to participate in new payment models. It encourages expansion of the APM options available to physicians, especially specialists, through physician-focused payment models (PFPMs). The law requires the establishment of a Technical Advisory Committee that will assess PFPM proposals submitted by stakeholders and make recommendations to the Secretary about which models to consider testing. Under the proposed rule, CMS would update this list annually to add new payment models that qualify to be an Advanced APM. In addition, starting in performance year 2019, clinicians could qualify for incentive payments based, in part, on participation in Advanced APMs developed by non-Medicare payers, such as private insurers or state Medicaid programs.

Medicare Part B Payments for Prescription Drugs

With concerns about the rapidly escalating prices of pharmaceuticals growing, CMS has initiated a controversial new demonstration program. Under Part B, physicians purchase drugs and then bill Medicare for prescription drugs administered in a physician's office or hospital outpatient department. Physicians and outpatient departments are typically paid the average sales price of a drug, plus a 6 percent add-on. Because they are ordered by physicians, some of the most expensive drugs are covered by Part B, such as those used to treat cancer, macular degeneration, and rheumatoid arthritis. Unlike Part D, Medicare's prescription drug program, Part B provides no incentives to provide lower cost treatments that are equally clinically effective. Justifications for the profit to physicians embedded in Part B payment are that it compensated for inadequate Medicare reimbursement, as for oncologists' services such as symptom management, psychosocial support, and end-of-life planning. However, there is evidence of substantial geographic variation in the administration and cost of Part B pharmaceuticals. Kavita Patel & Caitlin Brandt, A Controversial New Demonstration in Medicare: Potential Implications for Physician-Administered Drugs, Health Affs. Blog (May 3, 2016), http://healthaffairs.org/blog/2016/05/03/a-controversial-new-demonstration-in-medicare-potential-implications-for-physician-administered-drugs/.

CMS explained that its proposed rule is "designed to test different physician and patient incentives to do two things: drive the prescribing of the most effective drugs, and test new payment approaches to reward positive patient outcomes." CMS, Press Release (March 8, 2016), https://www.cms.gov/Newsroom/MediaReleaseDatabase/Press-releases/2016-Press-releases-items/2016-03-08.html. Under the proposed demonstration, the Part B add-on payment would be decreased to 2.5 percent plus a flat fee payment of $16.80 per drug per day. The proposed rule also includes several value-based pricing strategies and would discount or eliminate patient cost-sharing to improve Medicare beneficiaries' access to effective drugs. Dept. of Health & Human Servs. Medicare Program; Part D Drug Payment Model, 81 Fed. Reg. 13230 (March 11, 2016). A second phase of the demonstration would introduce reference pricing to Part B payment. CMS would set a standard payment rate for a group of "therapeutically similar" drugs. Pharmaceutical companies have opposed this method of pricing, asserting that patients with the same condition may respond differently to the same drug. Robert Pear, U.S. to Test Ways to Cut Drug Prices in Medicare, N.Y. Times (March 8, 2016), http://www.nytimes.com/2016/03/09/us/politics/us-to-test-ways-to-cut-drug-prices-in-medicare.html. In addition, CMS's proposal would institute value-based pricing which would vary prices for drugs based on clinical effectiveness.

What arguments might be leveled in opposition to the proposed rule? Does the fact that many Part B drugs are currently administered in doctors' offices rather than hospital facilities affect your analysis? Does value-based payment pose particular problems of administration in the case of pharmaceuticals?

6.   Fixing the Delivery System: ACOs, Pilots, Demonstrations, and Other New Things

   b.   Accountable Care Organizations (The Medicare Shared Savings Program)

Add at page 808 at end of first full paragraph:

   The market reaction to the original shared savings and Pioneer models of ACOs did not meet CMS's expectations. The great majority of ACOs elected to take the safer one-sided risk model, and the Pioneer model proved unattractive to some of the country's most advanced integrated delivery systems. Consequently, CMS has come forward with a third MSSP model, the "Next Generation" or Track 3 model. It includes several new features designed to appeal to providers willing to assume risk but under improved incentive features. The model employs prospectively-set benchmarks, and beneficiaries will choose to be aligned with the ACO. The goal is to determine whether stronger financial incentives for ACOs can improve health outcomes and reduce expenses of Medicare patients.

   The "Next Generation" model attempts to address what providers claim are three critical flaws in the design of the original MSSP: inadequate payment to cover start-up and administrative costs; the absence of incentives for patients to choose ACO providers; and the lack of ex ante notification to ACOs of the identity of patients they will be responsible for. The new model offers two risk arrangements: Risk Arrangement A offers shared savings and losses of up to 80%; Risk Arrangement B offers shared savings and losses of up to 100%. These are an increase from the Pioneer ACO option which entails savings and losses sharing up to 60–75%. Participating ACOs will receive their budgets prospectively so they can plan and manage care according to these targets from the beginning of the performance year. Moreover, under the new model, ACOs will have more tools to manage patient care, such as additional coverage of telehealth and post-discharge home services. Another notable change authorizes payments to beneficiaries for receiving care from ACOs. See CMS Next Generation ACO Model, https://innovation. cms.gov/initiatives/Next-Generation-ACO-Model/. CMS also took steps to give Track 1 ACOs additional time to transition to a two-sided performance-based risk program by allowing these ACOs to apply to renew for a second agreement period under the one-sided model.

   In January 2016, CMS announced that 21 organizations and companies had agreed to become Next Generation participants. While this number exceeds the number originally anticipated, some analysts believe the new program has cut into the Pioneer program, the original ACO demonstration program which has declined from the original 32 participants to 9. Bob Herman, New Medicare ACOs include First 'Next

Generation' Cohort, Mod. Healthcare (Jan. 11, 2016), http://www.modern
healthcare.com/article/20160111/NEWS/160119983.

III. MEDICAID

A. ELIGIBILITY

2. The ACA Medicaid Expansions

Add at page 838 at the end of subsection 2:

As of the summer of 2016, 32 states (including the District of
Columbia) have expanded Medicaid; 19 states have not done so.
http://kff.org/health-reform/state-indicator/state-activity-around-expanding-
medicaid-under-the-affordable-care-act/. Some states have expanded
Medicaid using section 1115 waivers that have allowed them to charge
premiums or impose cost sharing on some of the expansion population or
to enroll some through the marketplaces.

C. PAYMENT FOR SERVICES

3. Medicaid Managed Care

Add at page 855 at the end of subsection 3:

On April 25, 2016 HHS released a 1425-page final rule modernizing
managed care in Medicaid and the Children's Health Insurance Program
(CHIP). Thirty-nine states and the District of Columbia contract with
private managed care plans to furnish services to Medicaid beneficiaries,
and approximately three quarters of Medicaid beneficiaries are enrolled in
managed care. The rule is thus of major importance.

CMS described the rule as having four major goals: (1) supporting
states' efforts to advance delivery system reform and quality of care
improvements; (2) strengthening the consumer experience of care and
providing key consumer projections; (3) strengthening program integrity
by improving accountability and transparency; and (4) aligning rules
across health insurance coverage programs, including marketplace plans,
to improve efficiency and coverage transitions.

To support state efforts to reform delivery systems and improve
quality, the rule establishes a Medicaid Quality Rating System and
clarifies state authority to implement alternative payment models, pay
plans based on quality, and otherwise reform delivery systems. The rule
caps provider incentive payments and requires that they be conditioned on
actual performance and outcomes.

The rule attempts to strengthen the consumer experience of care by
improving managed care plan standards in the areas of enrollment,

disenrollment, communications, care coordination, and the availability and accessibility of covered services. It requires time and distance network adequacy standards in Medicaid and CHIP managed care for seven types of providers, although it leaves to the states responsibility for establishing the specific standards.

Some Medicaid managed care plans cover long term care. The Medicaid managed care rule establishes mechanisms for providing support, education, for managed care long-term care consumers. It prohibits intentional and de facto discrimination on the basis of health status, race, color, national origin, sex, sexual orientation, gender identity, or disability. It also establishes a central contact for complaints or concerns for beneficiaries, including assistance with enrollment, disenrollment, and the appeals process. It offers flexibility for plans to cover inpatient short-term mental health services, which have long been excluded from Medicaid coverage.

To promote accountability and strengthen program integrity, the rule requires additional transparency as to how Medicaid rates are set, including transparency with respect to data relating to utilization and quality of services. Payment rates must be actuarially sound and adequate to support the "efficient delivery" of care. The rule establishes a multi-factor methodology for rate development. It also requires standard contract terms covering issues like coverage of outpatient drugs, mental health parity, and limited free choice among providers.

To align rules across programs, the rule allows states to require reporting of medical loss ratios with the Medicare Advantage program and the marketplace and sets a target loss ratio of 85 percent, although it does not impose sanctions on insurers that fail to meet loss ratio targets, The rule also makes Medicaid plans' internal appeals processes and Medicaid's requirements for disseminating consumer information more similar to those that apply to private sector plans, including requirements for up-to-date provider directories.

The rule's provisions will be implemented in phases over the next three years, beginning on July 1, 2017. For further information on the rule see Sara Rosenbaum, Twenty-First Century Medicaid: the Final Managed Care Rule, http://healthaffairs.org/blog/2016/05/05/twenty-first-century-medicaid-the-final-managed-care-rule/, and Timothy Jost, Medicaid Managed Care Final Rule: Examining The Alignment with Qualified Health Plan Requirements, http://healthaffairs.org/blog/2016/04/29/medicaid-managed-care-final-rule-examining-the-alignment-with-qualified-health-plan-requirements/.

D. PROGRAM ADMINISTRATION AND FINANCING: FEDERAL/STATE RELATIONSHIPS

At page 864, replace Douglas v. Independent Living Center with the following case and Note:

ARMSTRONG V. EXCEPTIONAL CHILD CENTER, INC.

Supreme Court of the United States, 2015.
135 S.Ct. 1378.

JUSTICE SCALIA delivered the opinion of the Court, except as to Part IV.

We consider whether Medicaid providers can sue to enforce § (30)(A) of the Medicaid Act. 81 Stat. 911 (codified as amended at 42 U.S.C. § 1396a(a)(30)(A)).

I

Medicaid is a federal program that subsidizes the States' provision of medical services to "families with dependent children and of aged, blind, or disabled individuals, whose income and resources are insufficient to meet the costs of necessary medical services." [ ] Like other Spending Clause legislation, Medicaid offers the States a bargain: Congress provides federal funds in exchange for the States' agreement to spend them in accordance with congressionally imposed conditions.

In order to qualify for Medicaid funding, the State of Idaho adopted, and the Federal Government approved, a Medicaid "plan," [ ] which Idaho administers through its Department of Health and Welfare. Idaho's plan includes "habilitation services"—in-home care for individuals who, "but for the provision of such services . . . would require the level of care provided in a hospital or a nursing facility or intermediate care facility for the mentally retarded the cost of which could be reimbursed under the State plan," [ ] Providers of these services are reimbursed by the Department of Health and Welfare.

Section 30(A) of the Medicaid Act requires Idaho's plan to:

"provide such methods and procedures relating to the utilization of, and the payment for, care and services available under the plan . . . as may be necessary to safeguard against unnecessary utilization of such care and services and to assure that payments are consistent with efficiency, economy, and quality of care and are sufficient to enlist enough providers so that care and services are available under the plan at least to the extent that such care and services are available to the general population in the geographic area. . . ." [ ]

Respondents are providers of habilitation services to persons covered by Idaho's Medicaid plan. They sued petitioners—two officials in Idaho's Department of Health and Welfare—in the United States District Court for the District of Idaho, claiming that Idaho violates § 30(A) by reimbursing providers of habilitation services at rates lower than § 30(A) permits. They asked the court to enjoin petitioners to increase these rates.

The District Court entered summary judgment for the providers, holding that Idaho had not set rates in a manner consistent with § 30(A). [ ] The Ninth Circuit affirmed. [ ] It said that the providers had "an implied right of action under the Supremacy Clause to seek injunctive relief against the enforcement or implementation of state legislation." [ ] We granted certiorari. [ ]

II

The Supremacy Clause, Art. VI, cl. 2, reads:

> "This Constitution, and the Laws of the United States which shall be made in Pursuance thereof; and all Treaties made, or which shall be made, under the Authority of the United States, shall be the supreme Law of the Land; and the Judges in every State shall be bound thereby, any Thing in the Constitution or Laws of any State to the Contrary notwithstanding."

It is apparent that this Clause creates a rule of decision: Courts "shall" regard the "Constitution," and all laws "made in Pursuance thereof," as "the supreme Law of the Land." They must not give effect to state laws that conflict with federal laws. [ ] It is equally apparent that the Supremacy Clause is not the " 'source of any federal rights,' " [ ] and certainly does not create a cause of action. It instructs courts what to do when state and federal law clash, but is silent regarding who may enforce federal laws in court, and in what circumstances they may do so.

Hamilton wrote that the Supremacy Clause "only declares a truth, which flows immediately and necessarily from the institution of a Federal Government." [ ] And Story described the Clause as "a positive affirmance of that, which is necessarily implied." [ ] These descriptions would have been grossly inapt if the Clause were understood to give affected parties a constitutional (and hence congressionally unalterable) right to enforce federal laws against the States. And had it been understood to provide such significant private rights against the States, one would expect to find that mentioned in the preratification historical record, which contained ample discussion of the Supremacy Clause by both supporters and opponents of ratification. [ ] We are aware of no such mention, and respondents have not provided any. Its conspicuous absence militates strongly against their position.

Additionally, it is important to read the Supremacy Clause in the context of the Constitution as a whole. Article I vests Congress with broad discretion over the manner of implementing its enumerated powers, giving it authority to "make all Laws which shall be necessary and proper for carrying [them] into Execution." Art. I, § 8. * * * . It is unlikely that the Constitution gave Congress such broad discretion with regard to the enactment of laws, while simultaneously limiting Congress's power over the manner of their implementation, making it impossible to leave the enforcement of federal law to federal actors. If the Supremacy Clause includes a private right of action, then the Constitution requires Congress to permit the enforcement of its laws by private actors, significantly curtailing its ability to guide the implementation of federal law. * * *

To say that the Supremacy Clause does not confer a right of action is not to diminish the significant role that courts play in assuring the supremacy of federal law. For once a case or controversy properly comes before a court, judges are bound by federal law. Thus, a court may not convict a criminal defendant of violating a state law that federal law prohibits. [ ] Similarly, a court may not hold a civil defendant liable under state law for conduct federal law requires. [ ] And, as we have long recognized, if an individual claims federal law immunizes him from state regulation, the court may issue an injunction upon finding the state regulatory actions preempted. [ ]

Respondents contend that our preemption jurisprudence—specifically, the fact that we have regularly considered whether to enjoin the enforcement of state laws that are alleged to violate federal law— demonstrates that the Supremacy Clause creates a cause of action for its violation. They are incorrect. * * * What our cases demonstrate is that, "in a proper case, relief may be given in a court of equity . . . to prevent an injurious act by a public officer." [ ] The ability to sue to enjoin unconstitutional actions by state and federal officers is the creation of courts of equity, and reflects a long history of judicial review of illegal executive action, tracing back to England. [ ] It is a judge-made remedy, and we have never held or even suggested that, in its application to state officers, it rests upon an implied right of action contained in the Supremacy Clause. That is because, as even the dissent implicitly acknowledges, [ ] it does not. The Ninth Circuit erred in holding otherwise.

III

We turn next to respondents' contention that, quite apart from any cause of action conferred by the Supremacy Clause, this suit can proceed against Idaho in equity.

The power of federal courts of equity to enjoin unlawful executive action is subject to express and implied statutory limitations. [ ] " 'Courts of equity can no more disregard statutory and constitutional requirements and provisions than can courts of law.'" [] In our view the Medicaid Act implicitly precludes private enforcement of § 30(A), and respondents cannot, by invoking our equitable powers, circumvent Congress's exclusion of private enforcement. []

Two aspects of § 30(A) establish Congress's "intent to foreclose" equitable relief. [] First, the sole remedy Congress provided for a State's failure to comply with Medicaid's requirements—for the State's "breach" of the Spending Clause contract—is the withholding of Medicaid funds by the Secretary of Health and Human Services. [] * * *

The provision for the Secretary's enforcement by withholding funds might not, by itself, preclude the availability of equitable relief. [] But it does so when combined with the judicially unadministrable nature of § 30(A)'s text. It is difficult to imagine a requirement broader and less specific than § 30(A)'s mandate that state plans provide for payments that are "consistent with efficiency, economy, and quality of care," all the while "safeguard[ing] against unnecessary utilization of . . . care and services." Explicitly conferring enforcement of this judgment-laden standard upon the Secretary alone establishes, we think, that Congress "wanted to make the agency remedy that it provided exclusive," thereby achieving "the expertise, uniformity, widespread consultation, and resulting administrative guidance that can accompany agency decisionmaking," and avoiding "the comparative risk of inconsistent interpretations and misincentives that can arise out of an occasional inappropriate application of the statute in a private action." [] The sheer complexity associated with enforcing § 30(A), coupled with the express provision of an administrative remedy, [] shows that the Medicaid Act precludes private enforcement of § 30(A) in the courts.

The dissent agrees with us that the Supremacy Clause does not provide an implied right of action, and that Congress may displace the equitable relief that is traditionally available to enforce federal law. It disagrees only with our conclusion that such displacement has occurred here.

The dissent insists that, "because Congress is undoubtedly aware of the federal courts' long-established practice of enjoining preempted state action, it should generally be presumed to contemplate such enforcement unless it affirmatively manifests a contrary intent." [] But a "long-established practice" does not justify a rule that denies statutory text its fairest reading. Section 30(A), fairly read in the context of the Medicaid Act, "display[s] a[n] intent to foreclose" the availability of equitable relief. [] We have no warrant to revise Congress's scheme simply because it did not "affirmatively" preclude the availability of a judge-made action at equity. []

* * *

Finally, the dissent speaks as though we leave these plaintiffs with no resort. That is not the case. Their relief must be sought initially through the Secretary rather than through the courts. The dissent's complaint that the sanction available to the Secretary (the cut-off of funding) is too massive to be a realistic source of relief seems to us mistaken. We doubt that the Secretary's notice to a State that its compensation scheme is inadequate will be ignored.

IV

The last possible source of a cause of action for respondents is the Medicaid Act itself. They do not claim that, and rightly so. Section 30(A) lacks the sort of rights-creating language needed to imply a private right of action. [ ] It is phrased as a directive to the federal agency charged with approving state Medicaid plans, not as a conferral of the right to sue upon the beneficiaries of the State's decision to participate in Medicaid. The Act says that the "Secretary shall approve any plan which fulfills the conditions specified in subsection (a)," the subsection that includes § 30(A). [ ] We have held that such language "reveals no congressional intent to create a private right of action." [ ] And again, the explicitly conferred means of enforcing compliance with § 30(A) by the Secretary's withholding funding, [ ] suggests that other means of enforcement are precluded [ ].

Spending Clause legislation like Medicaid "is much in the nature of a contract." The notion that respondents have a right to sue derives, perhaps, from the fact that they are beneficiaries of the federal-state Medicaid agreement, and that intended beneficiaries, in modern times at least, can sue to enforce the obligations of private contracting parties. [ ] We doubt, to begin with, that providers are intended beneficiaries (as opposed to mere incidental beneficiaries) of the Medicaid agreement, which was concluded for the benefit of the infirm whom the providers were to serve, rather than for the benefit of the providers themselves. [ ] More fundamentally, however, the modern jurisprudence permitting intended beneficiaries to sue does not generally apply to contracts between a private party and the government, [ ] much less to contracts between two governments. Our precedents establish that a private right of action under federal law is not created by mere implication, but must be "unambiguously conferred," [ ] Nothing in the Medicaid Act suggests that Congress meant to change that for the commitments made under § 30(A).

* * *

The judgment of the Ninth Circuit Court of Appeals is reversed.

It is so ordered.

[JUSTICE BREYER concurred in the judgment and in the opinion in part and joined parts I, II, and III of the Court's opinion.]

JUSTICE SOTOMAYOR, with whom JUSTICE KENNEDY, JUSTICE GINSBURG, and JUSTICE KAGAN join, dissenting.

Suits in federal court to restrain state officials from executing laws that assertedly conflict with the Constitution or with a federal statute are not novel. To the contrary, this Court has adjudicated such requests for equitable relief since the early days of the Republic. Nevertheless, today the Court holds that Congress has foreclosed private parties from invoking the equitable powers of the federal courts to require States to comply with § 30(A) of the Medicaid Act, 42 U.S.C. § 1396a(a)(30)(A). It does so without pointing to the sort of detailed remedial scheme we have previously deemed necessary to establish congressional intent to preclude resort to equity. Instead, the Court relies on Congress' provision for agency enforcement of § 30(A)—an enforcement mechanism of the sort we have already definitively determined not to foreclose private actions—and on the mere fact that § 30(A) contains relatively broad language. As I cannot agree that these statutory provisions demonstrate the requisite congressional intent to restrict the equitable authority of the federal courts, I respectfully dissent.

Most important for purposes of this case is not the mere existence of this equitable authority, but the fact that it is exceedingly well established—supported, as the Court puts it, by a "long history." [ ] Congress may, if it so chooses, either expressly or implicitly preclude Ex parte Young enforcement actions with respect to a particular statute or category of lawsuit. [ ] But because Congress is undoubtedly aware of the federal courts' long-established practice of enjoining preempted state action, it should generally be presumed to contemplate such enforcement unless it affirmatively manifests a contrary intent. "Unless a statute in so many words, or by a necessary and inescapable inference, restricts the court's jurisdiction in equity, the full scope of that jurisdiction is to be recognized and applied." [ ] In this respect, equitable preemption actions differ from suits brought by plaintiffs invoking 42 U.S.C. § 1983 or an implied right of action to enforce a federal statute. Suits for "redress designed to halt or prevent the constitutional violation rather than the award of money damages" seek "traditional forms of relief." [ ]

By contrast, a plaintiff invoking § 1983 or an implied statutory cause of action may seek a variety of remedies—including damages—from a potentially broad range of parties. Rather than simply pointing to background equitable principles authorizing the action that Congress presumably has not overridden, such a plaintiff must demonstrate specific congressional intent to create a statutory right to these remedies. * * * For these reasons, the principles that we have developed to determine whether a statute creates an implied right of action, or is enforceable through § 1983, are not transferable to the Ex parte Young context.

* * *

[The dissent acknowledges that prior decisions have foreclosed an equitable action where there is an adequate remedy available.] What is the equivalent "carefully crafted and intricate remedial scheme" for enforcement of § 30(A)? The Court relies on two aspects of the Medicaid Act, but, whether considered separately or in combination, neither suffices.

First, the Court cites 42 U.S.C. § 1396c, which authorizes the Secretary of Health and Human Services (HHS) to withhold federal Medicaid payments to a State in whole or in part if the Secretary determines that the State has failed to comply with the obligations set out in § 1396a, including § 30(A). [ ] But * * * provides no specific procedure that parties actually affected by a State's violation of its statutory obligations may invoke in lieu of Ex parte Young—leaving them without any other avenue for seeking relief from the State. Nor will § 1396c always provide a particularly effective means for redressing a State's violations: If the State has violated § 30(A) by refusing to reimburse medical providers at a level "sufficient to enlist enough providers so that care and services are available" to Medicaid beneficiaries to the same extent as they are available to "the general population," agency action resulting in a reduced flow of federal funds to that State will often be self-defeating. [ ] Far from rendering § 1396c "superfluous," then, Ex parte Young actions would seem to be an anticipated and possibly necessary supplement to this limited agency-enforcement mechanism. * * *

* * *

Second, perhaps attempting to reconcile its treatment of § 1396c (2012 ed.) with this longstanding precedent, the Court focuses on the particular language of § 30(A), contending that this provision, at least, is so "judicially unadministrable" that Congress must have intended to preclude its enforcement in private suits. [ ]

Admittedly, the standard set out in § 30(A) is fairly broad, * * *

But mere breadth of statutory language does not require the Court to give up all hope of judicial enforcement—or, more important, to infer that Congress must have done so.

In fact, the contention that § 30(A)'s language was intended to foreclose private enforcement actions entirely is difficult to square with the provision's history. * * *

* * *

Of course, the broad scope of § 30(A)'s language is not irrelevant. But rather than compelling the conclusion that the provision is wholly unenforceable by private parties, its breadth counsels in favor of interpreting § 30(A) to provide substantial leeway to States, so that only in rare and extreme circumstances could a State actually be held to violate its mandate. The provision's scope may also often require a court to rely on HHS, which is "comparatively expert in the statute's subject matter." [ ] When the agency has made a determination with respect to what legal standard should apply, or the validity of a State's procedures for implementing its Medicaid plan, that determination should be accorded the appropriate deference. [ ] And if faced with a question that presents a special demand for agency expertise, a court might call for the views of the agency, or refer the question to the agency under the doctrine of primary jurisdiction. [ ] Finally, because the authority invoked for enforcing § 30(A) is equitable in nature, a plaintiff is not entitled to relief as of right, but only in the sound discretion of the court. [ ] Given the courts' ability to both respect States' legitimate choices and defer to the federal agency when necessary, I see no basis for presuming that Congress believed the Judiciary to be completely incapable of enforcing § 30(A).

* * *

The Court's error today has very real consequences. Previously, a State that set reimbursement rates so low that providers were unwilling to furnish a covered service for those who need it could be compelled by those affected to respect the obligation imposed by § 30(A). Now, it must suffice that a federal agency, with many programs to oversee, has authority to address such violations through the drastic and often counterproductive measure of withholding the funds that pay for such services. Because a faithful application of our precedents would have led to a contrary result, I respectfully dissent.

NOTE: THE MEDICAID PAYMENT RULE

On October 29, 2015, the Centers for Medicare and Medicaid Services of the Department of Health and Human Services released a final rule on "Methods for Assuring Access to Covered Medicaid Services." Although the rule had been proposed in 2011, CMS acknowledged that its release in 2015 was an explicit response to the *Armstrong* case, which, in rejecting a private cause of action to contest state Medicaid rates, had placed responsibility on CMS for ensuring that such rates are "consistent with efficiency, economy and quality of care" and to ensure sufficient beneficiary access to care under the program. The final rule was intended to strengthen CMS review and enforcement capabilities by requiring the states to provide more information to allow CMS to better monitor, measure, and ensure Medicaid access to care.

The final rule only applies to Medicaid fee-for-service payments. It does not apply to Medicaid managed care or to payments to providers through Medicaid managed care plans, although it does apply to services paid for on a fee-for-service basis carved out of managed care, such as behavioral health. The vast majority of Medicaid beneficiaries are currently enrolled through managed care plans. The rule also does not apply to Medicaid waiver and demonstration projects, which cover many more beneficiaries and providers.

The final rule establishes procedures that states must follow to receive CMS approval of provider rate reductions or rate restructurings that may negatively impact access to care. Before states reduce or restructure rates they must consider input from providers, beneficiaries, and other stakeholders. States must perform an analysis, considering comments received, regarding the effect of proposed rate changes on beneficiary access to care and must review and analyze program data developed under an access monitoring review plan before submitting proposed provider payment reductions and restructurings to CMS. States are also required to monitor the effect the changes have on access to care for at least three years after the changes are effective.

The final rule also imposes new CMS monitoring procedures on state fee for service payments in general. States must submit to CMS access monitoring review plans. To construct these access plans, states must specify data sources that support sufficient beneficiary access and that address:

- The extent to which beneficiary needs are met;

- The availability of care and providers;

- Changes in beneficiary service utilization; and

- Comparisons between Medicaid rates and rates paid by other public and private payers.

Access monitoring review plans must cover five services: primary care, physician specialists, behavioral health, pre- and post-natal obstetrics (including labor and delivery), and home health services. States may add additional services and must also monitor access for service for which payments have been reduced or restructured. If states or CMS receive a significantly high number of complaints about access to additional services, those will also be added to the review plan.

States must identify appropriate measures, data sources, baselines and thresholds for reviewing plans, taking into account state-specific delivery systems, beneficiary characteristics and needs, provider availability, and geography. CMS will not itself establish these standards but leaves it to the states. Review plans must be updated at least every three years. CMS requested additional comments on access review requirements and possible exemptions or alternatives. The rule does not prescribe remedial actions that must be taken if an access review reveals problems.

Finally, the final regulation requires states to implement ongoing mechanisms for beneficiary and provider input on access to care (through hotlines, surveys, ombudsman, or another equivalent mechanism). States must respond promptly to specific access problems identified through this input.

See Sara Rosenbaum, Medicaid and Access to Care: The Equal Access Rule, http://healthaffairs.org/blog/2015/11/19/medicaid-and-access-to-care-the-cms-equal-access-rule/.

CHAPTER 12

THE STRUCTURE OF THE HEALTH CARE ENTERPRISE

■ ■ ■

IV. TAX–EXEMPT HEALTH CARE ORGANIZATIONS

A. CHARITABLE PURPOSES: HOSPITALS

1. Exemption Under State Law

Add at page 1018 the following new Note 4:

4.   In a wide-ranging opinion, the New Jersey Tax Court stripped a hospital of most of its property tax exemption. AHS Hosp. Corp. v. Town of Morristown, 28 N.J. Tax 456 (2015). After surveying the complicated financial relationships of the hospital and its parent company, the court noted that if all nonprofit hospitals operated like Morristown Medical Center, then "for purposes of the property tax exemption, modern nonprofit hospitals are essentially legal fictions." Id. at 536. The court interpreted New Jersey's statute authorizing property tax exemptions as requiring a charitable function of the hospital rather than the hospital's mixture of for-profit and non-profit activities. The court found that the hospital failed the "profit test" under New Jersey law, emphasizing (1) the impossibility of determining which portions of the hospital were used by for-profit (non-employee) physicians and which were used by physicians employed by the hospital; (2) the ownership by the hospital's parent corporation of several for-profit companies (including one that was essentially an offshore bank account); and (3) the fact that trustees on the boards of the system's nonprofit entities often served as statutory officers for the for-profit companies.

The court was particularly troubled by the fact that non-employed physicians provided their services throughout the subject property and used the facility to generate bills which they charged patients directly, concluding that "by entangling its activities and operations with those of for-profit entities, the Hospital allowed its property to be used for profit." Doesn't this describe the practices of independent physicians at virtually all tax exempt hospitals? What policy complications flow from a requirement that exempt hospitals rely primarily or exclusively on employed physicians?

3. New Standards for Tax-Exempt Charitable Hospitals: IRC Section 501(r)

Add at page 1024 the following new Note 3:

3.   On December 29, 2014, the IRS issued its Final Rule implementing section 501(r). 79 Fed. Reg. 78954 (Dec. 31, 2014). An excellent summary and analysis of the regulations is Sara Rosenbaum, Additional Rules for Charitable Hospitals: Final Rules on Community Health Needs Assessment and Financial Assistance, Health Affs. Blog (Jan. 25, 2015). Some of the major provisions are described below:

- *Community Health Needs Assessment (CHNA)*. The rule makes clear that CHNAs must address not only the community's deficits in health care or access but also its health *needs*. The responsibility therefore extends to assessing social determinants of health including housing, environment, and nutrition. CMS emphasized the need to "prevent illness" and "address social, behavioral, and environmental factors that influence health in the community." Id. at 78963. The rule also stressed that CHNAs must assess the community that needs the hospital's care, not simply the hospital's current patients. Drawing a somewhat fuzzy line, the rule states that in defining its community, a hospital can take into account the geographic market it serves, its target populations, and its principal functions, but may not exclude various groups such as the medically underserved and low income populations or take into account the uninsured or publicly insured status of the community.

- *Financial Assistance*. The rules make clear that the financial assistance policy applies not only to emergency and medical care provided by the hospital but also to such care provided by "substantially related entities," such as partnerships with other entities. For entities that do not meet the substantially related test such as contracted organizations that are separate for tax purposes, the FAP must specify such relationships. Notably, where outsourcing occurs for emergency services and care is not covered by the FAP, the hospital may not claim such services as a community benefit under § 501(c)(3). As to what constitutes medically necessary care, the rule provides some flexibility, allowing hospitals to define the extent of such care, stating "a hospital facility may but is not required to use a definition of medically necessary care applicable under the laws of the state in which it is licensed, including the Medicaid definition, a definition that refers to the generally accepted standards of medicine in the community, or to an examining physician's determination."

- *Failure to Satisfy the Requirements of 501(r).* The rules give some guidance on when the "death penalty"—revocation of exempt status—will attach to noncompliance. The rule outlines a ten factor "facts and circumstances" test it will use to evaluate the potential seriousness of violations. This test takes into account the nature and scope of the failure, past conduct, the existence of a compliance plan at the time of the failure, and actions to correct and disclose the failure. "Minor omissions and errors" that are not cumulatively significant will not result in loss of exempt status, but prompt reporting and correction is expected. The excise tax may be imposed for failures to comply with individual requirements of the rules, although hospitals can avoid the tax via disclosure and correction.

- *Applicability.* Because the rules apply to individual hospitals, facility-specific compliance is required by entities controlling multiple hospitals. CMS declined to exempt government hospitals, and hospital organizations such as ACOs are also subject to the rules. However, the rules allow hospitals to voluntarily engage in joint CHNA development and to have joint FAPs as long as each facility separately adopts the policy. Finally, hospital-owned physician practices that are part of a hospital organization (and not separate taxable entities) are subject to both the CHNA and financial assistance obligations.

C. CHARITABLE PURPOSES: INTEGRATED DELIVERY SYSTEMS

Add at page 1039 at the end of Note 5:

On April 8, 2016, the IRS issued a private letter ruling denying tax-exempt section 501(c)(3) status to a nonprofit accountable care organization that did not participate in the Medicare Shared Savings Program ("MSSP"). I.R.S. Priv. Ltr. Ruling 201615022 (Jan. 15, 2016). The ACO was formed by a nonprofit tax-exempt health care system ("System") in order to promote clinical care integration, coordination, and accountability among physicians practicing throughout the System's affiliated facilities. The ACO apparently argued that it merited exempt status because time and resources were dedicated to the "triple aim" of the program: (1) reducing the cost of health care for individuals; (2) improving patient access to, and the quality of, healthcare; and (3) improving population health and patient experience. The ACO's integrated network of health care providers included: (i) physicians employed by the System and its facilities; (ii) physicians from independent practice groups that were members of the medical staff at System affiliated facilities; and (iii) physicians practicing at non-System affiliated hospitals and in other healthcare systems. However, one-half of the participating physicians were members of independent practice groups or otherwise unaffiliated with the System. The ACO collected, analyzed, and warehoused data and also served as the representative for all participating providers, including independent and non-System affiliated physicians, in negotiating and executing agreements with third-party payers. Importantly, the ACO did not participate in the MSSP.

The IRS concluded that the ACO was not operated "exclusively" for section 501(c)(3) purposes, finding that it did not in any way lessen the burdens of government by negotiating with third-party payers outside of the MSSP and was not engaged primarily in assisting the Medicare or Medicaid population. While acknowledging that the promotion of health has been recognized as a charitable activity, the IRS found that the ACO's negotiation of third-party payer agreements on behalf of independent and non-System affiliated physicians was not a charitable activity. Because the non-charitable activity comprised a substantial part of the ACO's activities and conferred an impermissible private benefit to the unaffiliated physicians and the private benefit was substantial, the IRS found that the ACO did not qualify for exemption under section 501(c)(3). Moreover, because the ACO's activities were not exclusively for the benefit of the System, the IRS found that the ACO, even if it had qualified for exemption under section 501(c)(3), would not qualify as a supporting organization and would be considered a private foundation.

The ruling does not change the IRS's position that an ACO engaged exclusively in MSSP activities can qualify for section 501(c)(3) status, provided the other organizational and operational requirements of section 501(c)(3) are satisfied. What is made clear is that the IRS will not grant section 501(c)(3) status to an ACO engaged primarily in non-MSSP activities on behalf of health care providers that are non-section 501(c)(3) organizations. What remains uncertain is under what circumstances can an ACO engaged in both MSSP and non-MSSP activities qualify for tax-exempt status and, if so, to what extent could the ACO perform non-MSSP activities on behalf of non-section 501(c)(3) organizations or physicians employed by such organizations. The American Hospital Association responded quickly to the PLR, stating the ruling is "in conflict with the direction that [HHS] has given to the hospital field" and asking the IRS to publish guidance affirming that "hospitals may participate in ACOs without generating a tax cost or incurring the catastrophic loss of their tax-exempt status." Letter from Melinda Reid Hatton, General Counsel, American Hospital Ass'n to Mark Mazur, Ass't Secretary, Dep't of the Treasury (May 16, 2016).

CHAPTER 13

FRAUD AND ABUSE

■ ■ ■

I. FALSE CLAIMS

A. GOVERNMENTAL ENFORCEMENT

At page 1090, replace United States ex rel. Mikes v. Straus with the following case:

UNIVERSAL HEALTH SERVICES, INC. V. UNITED STATES ET AL. EX REL. ESCOBAR ET AL.

Supreme Court of the United States, 2016.
136 S.Ct. 1989.

THOMAS, J., delivered the opinion for a unanimous Court.

Opinion

JUSTICE THOMAS delivered the opinion of the Court.

The False Claims Act, [ ] imposes significant penalties on those who defraud the Government. This case concerns a theory of False Claims Act liability commonly referred to as "implied false certification." According to this theory, when a defendant submits a claim, it impliedly certifies compliance with all conditions of payment. But if that claim fails to disclose the defendant's violation of a material statutory, regulatory, or contractual requirement, so the theory goes, the defendant has made a misrepresentation that renders the claim "false or fraudulent" under § 3729(a)(1)(A). This case requires us to consider this theory of liability and to clarify some of the circumstances in which the False Claims Act imposes liability.

We first hold that, at least in certain circumstances, the implied false certification theory can be a basis for liability. Specifically, liability can attach when the defendant submits a claim for payment that makes specific representations about the goods or services provided, but knowingly fails to disclose the defendant's noncompliance with a statutory, regulatory, or contractual requirement. In these circumstances, liability may attach if the omission renders those representations misleading.

We further hold that False Claims Act liability for failing to disclose violations of legal requirements does not turn upon whether those requirements were expressly designated as conditions of payment. Defendants can be liable for violating requirements even if they were not expressly designated as conditions of payment. Conversely, even when a requirement is expressly designated a condition of payment, not every violation of such a requirement gives rise to liability. What matters is not the label the Government attaches to a requirement, but whether the defendant knowingly violated a requirement that the defendant knows is material to the Government's payment decision.

A misrepresentation about compliance with a statutory, regulatory, or contractual requirement must be material to the Government's payment decision in order to be actionable under the False Claims Act. We clarify below how that rigorous materiality requirement should be enforced.

Because the courts below interpreted § 3729(a)(1)(A) differently, we vacate the judgment and remand so that those courts may apply the approach set out in this opinion.

* * *

B

The alleged False Claims Act violations here arose within the Medicaid program, a joint state-federal program in which healthcare providers serve poor or disabled patients and submit claims for government reimbursement. [ ] The facts recited in the complaint, which we take as true at this stage, are as follows. For five years, Yarushka Rivera, a teenage beneficiary of Massachusetts' Medicaid program, received counseling services at Arbour Counseling Services, a satellite mental health facility in Lawrence, Massachusetts, owned and operated by a subsidiary of petitioner Universal Health Services. Beginning in 2004, when Yarushka started having behavioral problems, five medical professionals at Arbour intermittently treated her. In May 2009, Yarushka had an adverse reaction to a medication that a purported doctor at Arbour prescribed after diagnosing her with bipolar disorder. Her condition worsened; she suffered a seizure that required hospitalization. In October 2009, she suffered another seizure and died. She was 17 years old.

Thereafter, an Arbour counselor revealed to respondents Carmen Correa and Julio Escobar—Yarushka's mother and stepfather—that few Arbour employees were actually licensed to provide mental health counseling and that supervision of them was minimal. Respondents discovered that, of the five professionals who had treated Yarushka, only one was properly licensed. The practitioner who diagnosed Yarushka as bipolar identified herself as a psychologist with a Ph. D., but failed to mention that her degree came from an unaccredited Internet college and that Massachusetts had rejected her application to be licensed as a psychologist. Likewise, the practitioner who prescribed medicine to

Yarushka, and who was held out as a psychiatrist, was in fact a nurse who lacked authority to prescribe medications absent supervision. Rather than ensuring supervision of unlicensed staff, the clinic's director helped to misrepresent the staff's qualifications. And the problem went beyond those who treated Yarushka. Some 23 Arbour employees lacked licenses to provide mental health services, yet—despite regulatory requirements to the contrary—they counseled patients and prescribed drugs without supervision.

When submitting reimbursement claims, Arbour used payment codes corresponding to different services that its staff provided to Yaruskha, such as "Individual Therapy" and "family therapy." [ ] Staff members also misrepresented their qualifications and licensing status to the Federal Government to obtain individual National Provider Identification numbers, which are submitted in connection with Medicaid reimbursement claims and correspond to specific job titles. For instance, one Arbour staff member who treated Yaruskha registered for a number associated with "Social Worker, Clinical," despite lacking the credentials and licensing required for social workers engaged in mental health counseling. [ ]

After researching Arbour's operations, respondents filed complaints with various Massachusetts agencies. Massachusetts investigated and ultimately issued a report detailing Arbour's violation of over a dozen Massachusetts Medicaid regulations governing the qualifications and supervision required for staff at mental health facilities. Arbour agreed to a remedial plan, and two Arbour employees also entered into consent agreements with Massachusetts.

In 2011, respondents filed a *qui tam* suit in federal court, alleging that Universal Health had violated the False Claims Act under an implied false certification theory of liability. The operative complaint asserts that Universal Health (acting through Arbour) submitted reimbursement claims that made representations about the specific services provided by specific types of professionals, but that failed to disclose serious violations of regulations pertaining to staff qualifications and licensing requirements for these services. Specifically, the Massachusetts Medicaid program requires satellite facilities to have specific types of clinicians on staff, delineates licensing requirements for particular positions (like psychiatrists, social workers, and nurses), and details supervision requirements for other staff. [ ] Universal Health allegedly flouted these regulations because Arbour employed unqualified, unlicensed, and unsupervised staff. The Massachusetts Medicaid program, unaware of these deficiencies, paid the claims. Universal Health thus allegedly defrauded the program, which would not have reimbursed the claims had it known that it was billed for mental health services that were performed by unlicensed and unsupervised staff. The United States declined to intervene.

[The District Court granted Universal Health's motion to dismiss the complaint, finding that although the First Circuit precedent had previously embraced the implied false certification theory of liability, respondents had failed to state a claim because the regulations were not a condition of payment. Reversing the district court, the First Circuit held that a statutory, regulatory, or contractual requirement can be a condition of payment either by expressly identifying itself as such or by implication. It concluded that the Massachusetts Medicaid regulations "clearly impose conditions of payment" and held that the regulations themselves "constitute[d] dispositive evidence of materiality," because they identified adequate supervision as an "express and absolute" condition of payment and "repeated[ly] reference[d]" supervision.]

We granted certiorari to resolve the disagreement among the Courts of Appeals over the validity and scope of the implied false certification theory of liability. [ ] The Seventh Circuit has rejected this theory, reasoning that only express (or affirmative) falsehoods can render a claim "false or fraudulent" under 31 U. S. C. § 3729(a)(1)(A). [ ] Other courts have accepted the theory, but limit its application to cases where defendants fail to disclose violations of expressly designated conditions of payment. *E.g., Mikes v. Straus*, 274 F. 3d 687, 700 (CA2 2011). Yet others hold that conditions of payment need not be expressly designated as such to be a basis for False Claims Act liability. [ ]

II

We first hold that the implied false certification theory can, at least in some circumstances, provide a basis for liability. By punishing defendants who submit "false or fraudulent claims," the False Claims Act encompasses claims that make fraudulent misrepresentations, which include certain misleading omissions. When, as here, a defendant makes representations in submitting a claim but omits its violations of statutory, regulatory, or contractual requirements, those omissions can be a basis for liability if they render the defendant's representations misleading with respect to the goods or services provided.

To reach this conclusion, "[w]e start, as always, with the language of the statute." [ ] The False Claims Act imposes civil liability on "any person who . . . knowingly presents, or causes to be presented, a false or fraudulent claim for payment or approval." [ ] Congress did not define what makes a claim "false" or "fraudulent." But "[i]t is a settled principle of interpretation that, absent other indication, Congress intends to incorporate the well-settled meaning of the common-law terms it uses." [ ]

Because common-law fraud has long encompassed certain misrepresentations by omission, "false or fraudulent claims" include more than just claims containing express falsehoods. The parties and the

Government agree that misrepresentations by omission can give rise to liability. [ ]

The parties instead dispute whether submitting a claim without disclosing violations of statutory, regulatory, or contractual requirements constitutes such an actionable misrepresentation. Respondents and the Government invoke the common-law rule that, while nondisclosure alone ordinarily is not actionable, "[a] representation stating the truth so far as it goes but which the maker knows or believes to be materially misleading because of his failure to state additional or qualifying matter" is actionable. Restatement (Second) of Torts § 529, p. 62 (1976). They contend that every submission of a claim for payment implicitly represents that the claimant is legally entitled to payment, and that failing to disclose violations of material legal requirements renders the claim misleading. Universal Health, on the other hand, argues that submitting a claim involves no representations, and that a different common-law rule thus governs: nondisclosure of legal violations is not actionable absent a special "duty . . . to exercise reasonable care to disclose the matter in question," which it says is lacking in Government contracting. [ ]

We need not resolve whether all claims for payment implicitly represent that the billing party is legally entitled to payment. The claims in this case do more than merely demand payment. They fall squarely within the rule that half-truths—representations that state the truth only so far as it goes, while omitting critical qualifying information—can be actionable misrepresentations. . . .

So too here, by submitting claims for payment using payment codes that corresponded to specific counseling services, Universal Health represented that it had provided individual therapy, family therapy, preventive medication counseling, and other types of treatment. Moreover, Arbour staff members allegedly made further representations in submitting Medicaid reimbursement claims by using National Provider Identification numbers corresponding to specific job titles. And these representations were clearly misleading in context. Anyone informed that a social worker at a Massachusetts mental health clinic provided a teenage patient with individual counseling services would probably—but wrongly— conclude that the clinic had complied with core Massachusetts Medicaid requirements (1) that a counselor "treating children [is] required to have specialized training and experience in children's services," [ ] and also (2) that, at a minimum, the social worker possesses the prescribed qualifications for the job [ ]. By using payment and other codes that conveyed this information without disclosing Arbour's many violations of basic staff and licensing requirements for mental health facilities, Universal Health's claims constituted misrepresentations.

Accordingly, we hold that the implied certification theory can be a basis for liability, at least where two conditions are satisfied: first, the claim does not merely request payment, but also makes specific representations about the goods or services provided; and second, the defendant's failure to disclose noncompliance with material statutory, regulatory, or contractual requirements makes those representations misleading half-truths.

III

The second question presented is whether, as Universal Health urges, a defendant should face False Claims Act liability only if it fails to disclose the violation of a contractual, statutory, or regulatory provision that the Government expressly designated a condition of payment. We conclude that the Act does not impose this limit on liability. But we also conclude that not every undisclosed violation of an express condition of payment automatically triggers liability. Whether a provision is labeled a condition of payment is relevant to but not dispositive of the materiality inquiry.

A

Nothing in the text of the False Claims Act supports Universal Health's proposed restriction. Section 3729(a)(1)(A) imposes liability on those who present "false or fraudulent claims" but does not limit such claims to misrepresentations about express conditions of payment. See *SAIC*, 626 F. 3d, at 1268 (rejecting any textual basis for an express-designation rule). Nor does the common-law meaning of fraud tether liability to violating an express condition of payment. A statement that misleadingly omits critical facts is a misrepresentation irrespective of whether the other party has expressly signaled the importance of the qualifying information. [ ]

The False Claims Act's materiality requirement also does not support Universal Health. Under the Act, the misrepresentation must be material to the other party's course of action. But, as discussed below, [ ], statutory, regulatory, and contractual requirements are not automatically material, even if they are labeled conditions of payment. [ ]

Nor does the Act's scienter requirement [ ] support Universal Health's position. A defendant can have "actual knowledge" that a condition is material without the Government expressly calling it a condition of payment. If the Government failed to specify that guns it orders must actually shoot, but the defendant knows that the Government routinely rescinds contracts if the guns do not shoot, the defendant has "actual knowledge." Likewise, because a reasonable person would realize the imperative of a functioning firearm, a defendant's failure to appreciate the materiality of that condition would amount to "deliberate ignorance" or "reckless disregard" of the "truth or falsity of the information" even if the Government did not spell this out.

Universal Health nonetheless contends that False Claims Act liability should be limited to undisclosed violations of expressly designated conditions of payment to provide defendants with fair notice and to cabin liability. But policy arguments cannot supersede the clear statutory text. [ ] In any event, Universal Health's approach risks undercutting these policy goals. The Government might respond by designating every legal requirement an express condition of payment. But billing parties are often subject to thousands of complex statutory and regulatory provisions. Facing False Claims Act liability for violating any of them would hardly help would-be defendants anticipate and prioritize compliance obligations. And forcing the Government to expressly designate a provision as a condition of *payment* would create further arbitrariness. Under Universal Health's view, misrepresenting compliance with a requirement that the Government expressly identified as a condition of payment could expose a defendant to liability. Yet, under this theory, misrepresenting compliance with a condition of eligibility to even participate in a federal program when submitting a claim would not.

Moreover, other parts of the False Claims Act allay Universal Health's concerns. "[I]nstead of adopting a circumscribed view of what it means for a claim to be false or fraudulent," concerns about fair notice and open-ended liability "can be effectively addressed through strict enforcement of the Act's materiality and scienter requirements." [ ] Those requirements are rigorous.

B

As noted, a misrepresentation about compliance with a statutory, regulatory, or contractual requirement must be material to the Government's payment decision in order to be actionable under the False Claims Act. We now clarify how that materiality requirement should be enforced.

Section 3729(b)(4) defines materiality using language that we have employed to define materiality in other federal fraud statutes: "[T]he term 'material' means having a natural tendency to influence, or be capable of influencing, the payment or receipt of money or property." See *Neder*, 527 U.S., at 16 (using this definition to interpret the mail, bank, and wire fraud statutes); *Kungys v. United States*, 485 U.S. 759, 770 (1988) (same for fraudulent statements to immigration officials). This materiality requirement descends from "common-law antecedents." [ ] Indeed, "the common law could not have conceived of 'fraud' without proof of materiality." [ ]

We need not decide whether § 3729(a)(1)(A)'s materiality requirement is governed by § 3729(b)(4) or derived directly from the common law. Under any understanding of the concept, materiality "look[s] to the effect on the

likely or actual behavior of the recipient of the alleged misrepresentation."
. . .

The materiality standard is demanding. The False Claims Act is not "an all-purpose antifraud statute," [ ] or a vehicle for punishing garden-variety breaches of contract or regulatory violations. A misrepresentation cannot be deemed material merely because the Government designates compliance with a particular statutory, regulatory, or contractual requirement as a condition of payment. Nor is it sufficient for a finding of materiality that the Government would have the option to decline to pay if it knew of the defendant's noncompliance. Materiality, in addition, cannot be found where noncompliance is minor or insubstantial. . . .

In sum, when evaluating materiality under the False Claims Act, the Government's decision to expressly identify a provision as a condition of payment is relevant, but not automatically dispositive. Likewise, proof of materiality can include, but is not necessarily limited to, evidence that the defendant knows that the Government consistently refuses to pay claims in the mine run of cases based on noncompliance with the particular statutory, regulatory, or contractual requirement. Conversely, if the Government pays a particular claim in full despite its actual knowledge that certain requirements were violated, that is very strong evidence that those requirements are not material. Or, if the Government regularly pays a particular type of claim in full despite actual knowledge that certain requirements were violated, and has signaled no change in position, that is strong evidence that the requirements are not material.[6]

These rules lead us to disagree with the Government's and First Circuit's view of materiality: that any statutory, regulatory, or contractual violation is material so long as the defendant knows that the Government would be entitled to refuse payment were it aware of the violation. [ ] If the Government contracts for health services and adds a requirement that contractors buy American-made staplers, anyone who submits a claim for those services but fails to disclose its use of foreign staplers violates the False Claims Act. To the Government, liability would attach if the defendant's use of foreign staplers would entitle the Government not to pay the claim in whole or part—irrespective of whether the Government routinely pays claims despite knowing that foreign staplers were used. [ ] Likewise, if the Government required contractors to aver their compliance with the entire U.S. Code and Code of Federal Regulations, then under this view, failing to mention noncompliance with any of those requirements

---

[6] We reject Universal Health's assertion that materiality is too fact intensive for courts to dismiss False Claims Act cases on a motion to dismiss or at summary judgment. The standard for materiality that we have outlined is a familiar and rigorous one. And False Claims Act plaintiffs must also plead their claims with plausibility and particularity under Federal Rules of Civil Procedure 8 and 9(b) by, for instance, pleading facts to support allegations of materiality.

would always be material. The False Claims Act does not adopt such an extraordinarily expansive view of liability.

* * *

Because both opinions below assessed respondents' complaint based on interpretations of § 3729(a)(1)(A) that differ from ours, we vacate the First Circuit's judgment and remand the case for reconsideration of whether respondents have sufficiently pleaded a False Claims Act violation. [ ] We emphasize, however, that the False Claims Act is not a means of imposing treble damages and other penalties for insignificant regulatory or contractual violations. This case centers on allegations of fraud, not medical malpractice. Respondents have alleged that Universal Health misrepresented its compliance with mental health facility requirements that are so central to the provision of mental health counseling that the Medicaid program would not have paid these claims had it known of these violations. Respondents may well have adequately pleaded a violation of § 3729(a)(1)(A). But we leave it to the courts below to resolve this in the first instance.

The judgment of the Court of Appeals is vacated, and the case is remanded for further proceedings consistent with this opinion.

III. THE STARK LAW: A TRANSACTIONAL APPROACH TO SELF–REFERRALS

B. EXCEPTIONS

Add at page 1150 the following new Note preceding but not replacing Note 1 and renumber the existing Notes:

1. *Rules reducing risk for technical "foot fault" violations.* On November 16, 2015, CMS published the Medicare Physician Fee Schedule Final Rule that includes a final rule which "updates the physician self-referral regulations to accommodate delivery and payment system reform, to reduce burden, and to facilitate compliance." 80 Fed. Reg. 70,886, 71,301. The rule includes a number of significant provisions relaxing technical requirements that have ensnared many physicians. For example, as noted in the text, exceptions for physicians with compensation arrangements impose specific requirements for space leases, equipment leases, employment compensation, personal services arrangements, physician recruitment incentives, and physician retention incentives, such as that the compensation to the physician be set in advance, fair market value, and not determined in a manner that takes into account the volume or value of referrals or other business generated by the physician. The new rule modifies and clarifies these requirements as follows:

- Clarifying that signed writings need not be formal contractual agreements and that the one-year term requirement can be evidenced by "a collection of documents, including contemporaneous documents evidencing the course of conduct between the parties."

- Extending the provisions that had protected "holdover" arrangements from a six-month period to protect holdovers indefinitely, provided certain requirements are met, such as that rental arrangements must continue to satisfy all elements of exceptions (e.g., consistency with fair market value) over time.

- Clarifying how the signed writing and volume/value standards apply when direct compensation arrangements arise from the "stand in the shoes" rule.

Getting even deeper into the weeds, the rule also addressed an issue arising out of an important setback the agency faced in court. In Council for Urological Interests v. Burwell, 790 F.3d 219 (D.C. Cir. 2015), the U.S. Court of Appeals for the District of Columbia Circuit upheld a CMS rule which redefined an "entity furnishing designated health services" to include entities that perform the services, not just bill for them. However, the D.C. Circuit also held that CMS's prohibition on "per-click" equipment rental arrangements by physician-owned leasing companies lacked a rational basis based on the agency's "tortured reading" of a Congressional conference report regarding the statutory exception. The court remanded the case, stating that the Secretary of HHS "should consider—with more care than she exercised here—whether a per-click ban on equipment leases is consistent with the 1993 Conference Report."

This led to speculation as to whether the Secretary would take alternative action to addressing per-unit-of-service arrangements, including invoking Anti-Kickback statute. Notably in the proposed rulemaking, the agency found another avenue to address the issue. The new rule creates a new exception for timeshare arrangements that would permit arrangements where a physician obtains the right to use premises, equipment, personnel, items, supplies or services on a limited or as-needed basis. See § 411.357(y). In restricting per-unit-of-service compensation under the timeshare exception, CMS stated that, in its view, the court's decision in *Urological Interests* does not prevent CMS from restricting per-unit-of-service compensation under all circumstances. Hence, it prohibited such arrangements under the new timeshare exception based on its authority under section 1877(e)(1)(B)(vi) to promulgate "other requirements" by regulation as needed to protect against program or patient abuse.

Add at page 1153 after Note 3:

The following decision of the Fourth Circuit resolved the appeal of the Tuomey case discussed in Note 3.

UNITED STATES EX REL. MICHAEL K. DRAKEFORD V. TUOMEY

United States Court of Appeals, Fourth Circuit, 2015.
792 F.3d 364.

DIAZ, CIRCUIT JUDGE:

In a qui tam action in which the government intervened, a jury determined that Tuomey Healthcare System, Inc., did not violate the False Claims Act ("FCA") [ ]. The district court, however, vacated the jury's verdict and granted the government a new trial after concluding that it had erroneously excluded excerpts of a Tuomey executive's deposition testimony. The jury in the second trial found that Tuomey knowingly submitted 21,730 false claims to Medicare for reimbursement. The district court then entered final judgment for the government and awarded damages and civil penalties totaling $237,454,195.

Tuomey contends that the district court erred in granting the government's motion for a new trial. Tuomey also lodges numerous other challenges to the judgment entered against it following the second trial. It argues that it is entitled to judgment as a matter of law (or, in the alternative, yet another new trial) because it did not violate the FCA. In the alternative, Tuomey asks for a new trial because the district court failed to properly instruct the jury. Finally, Tuomey asks us to strike the damages and civil penalties award as either improperly calculated or unconstitutional.

We conclude that the district court correctly granted the government's motion for a new trial, albeit for a reason different than that relied upon by the district court. We also reject Tuomey's claims of error following the second trial. Accordingly, we affirm the district court's judgment.

I

A

Tuomey is a nonprofit hospital located in Sumter, South Carolina, a small, largely rural community that is a federally-designated medically underserved area. At the time of the events leading up to this lawsuit, most of the physicians that practiced at Tuomey were not directly employed by the hospital, but instead were members of independent specialty practices.

Beginning around 2000, doctors who previously performed outpatient surgery at Tuomey began doing so in their own offices or at off-site surgery centers. The loss of this revenue stream was a source of grave concern for Tuomey because it collected substantial facility fees from patients who underwent surgery at the hospital's outpatient center. Tuomey estimated that it stood to lose $8 to $12 million over a thirteen-year period from the loss of fees associated with gastrointestinal procedures alone. To stem this loss, Tuomey sought to negotiate part-time employment contracts with a number of local physicians.

* * *

Beginning in 2003, Tuomey sought the advice of its longtime counsel, Nexsen Pruet, on the Stark Law implications arising from the proposed employment contracts. Nexsen Pruet in turn engaged Cejka Consulting, a national consulting firm that specialized in physician compensation, to provide an opinion concerning the commercial reasonableness and fair market value of the contracts. Tuomey also conferred with Richard Kusserow, a former Inspector General for the United States Department of Health and Human Services, and later, with Steve Pratt, an attorney at Hall Render, a prominent healthcare law firm.

The part-time employment contracts had substantially similar terms. Each physician was paid an annual guaranteed base salary. That salary was adjusted from year to year based on the amount the physician collected from all services rendered the previous year. The bulk of the physicians' compensation was earned in the form of a productivity bonus, which paid the physicians eighty percent of the amount of their collections for that year. The physicians were also eligible for an incentive bonus of up to seven percent of their earned productivity bonus. In addition, Tuomey agreed to pay for the physicians' medical malpractice liability insurance as well as their practice group's share of employment taxes. The physicians were also allowed to participate in Tuomey's health insurance plan. Finally, Tuomey agreed to absorb each practice group's billing and collections costs.

The contracts had ten-year terms, during which physicians could maintain their private practices, but were required to perform outpatient surgical procedures exclusively at the hospital. Physicians could not own any interest in a facility located in Sumter that provided ambulatory surgery services, save for a less-than-two-percent interest in a publicly traded company that provided such services. The physicians also agreed not to perform outpatient surgical procedures within a thirty-mile radius of the hospital for two years after the expiration or termination of the contracts.

Tuomey ultimately entered into part-time employment contracts with nineteen physicians. Tuomey, however, was unable to reach an agreement with Dr. Michael Drakeford, an orthopedic surgeon. Drakeford believed that the proposed contracts violated the Stark Law because the physicians were being paid in excess of their collections. He contended that the compensation package did not reflect fair market value, and thus the government would view it as an unlawful payment for the doctor's facility-fee-generating referrals.

* * *

Unable to break the stalemate in their negotiations, in May 2005, Tuomey and Drakeford sought the advice of Kevin McAnaney, an attorney in private practice with expertise in the Stark Law. McAnaney had formerly served as the Chief of the Industry Guidance Branch of the United States Department of Health and Human Services Office of Counsel to the Inspector General. In that position, McAnaney wrote a "substantial portion" of the regulations implementing the Stark Law.

McAnaney advised the parties that the proposed employment contracts raised significant "red flags" under the Stark Law.[2] [ ] In particular, Tuomey would have serious difficulty persuading the government that the contracts did not compensate the physicians in excess of fair market value. Such a contention, said McAnaney, would not pass the "red face test." [ ] McAnaney also warned Tuomey that the contracts presented "an easy case to prosecute" for the government. [ ]

Drakeford ultimately declined to enter into a contract with Tuomey. He later sued the hospital under the qui tam provisions of the FCA, alleging that because the part-time employment contracts violated the Stark Law, Tuomey had knowingly submitted false claims for payment to Medicare. As was its right, the government intervened in the action and filed additional claims seeking equitable relief for payments made under mistake of fact and unjust enrichment theories.

* * *

II

A

Tuomey's appeal presents these issues: First, did the district court err in granting the government's motion for a new trial on the FCA claim? If not, did the district court err in (1) denying Tuomey's motion for judgment as a matter of law (or, in the alternative, for yet another new trial) following the second trial; and (2) awarding damages and penalties against Tuomey based on the jury's finding of an FCA violation? We address each issue in turn, but first provide a general overview of the Stark Law.

B

The Stark Law is intended to prevent "overutilization of services by physicians who [stand] to profit from referring patients to facilities or entities in which they [have] a financial interest." [ ] The statute prohibits a physician from making a referral to an entity, such as a hospital, with which he or she has a financial relationship, for the furnishing of designated health services. [ ] If the physician makes such a referral, the hospital may not submit a bill for reimbursement to Medicare. [ ] Similarly, the government may not make any payment for a designated health service provided in violation of the Stark Law. [ ] If a person collects any payment

---

[2] According to McAnaney, the joint venture alternative raised separate concerns under the Anti-Kickback Statute [ ] which bars "the payment of remuneration for the purpose of inducing the purchase of health care covered by any federal health care insurance program." [ ]

for a service billed in violation of the Stark Law, "the person shall be liable to the individual for, and shall refund on a timely basis to the individual, any amounts so collected." [ ]4

Inpatient and outpatient hospital services are considered designated health services under the law. [ ] A referral includes "the request by a physician for the item or service." [ ] A referral does not include "any designated health service personally performed or provided by the referring physician." [ ] However, there is a referral when the hospital bills a "facility fee" (also known as a "facility component" or "technical component") "in connection with the personally performed service." [ ]

A financial relationship constitutes a prohibited "indirect compensation arrangement," if (1) "there exists an unbroken chain of any number . . . of persons or entities that have financial relationships . . . between them," (2) "[t]he referring physician . . . receives aggregate compensation . . . that varies with, or takes into account, the volume or value of referrals or other business generated by the referring physician for the entity furnishing" the designated health services, and (3) the entity has knowledge that the compensation so varies. [ ] *see also Drakeford,* 675 F.3d at 408 ("[C]ompensation arrangements that take into account anticipated referrals . . . implicate the volume or value standard."). The statute, however, does not bar indirect compensation arrangements where: (1) the referring physician is compensated at fair market value for "services and items actually provided"; (2) the compensation arrangement is "not determined in any manner that takes into account the volume or value of referrals"; (3) the compensation arrangement is "commercially reasonable"; and (4) the compensation arrangement does not run afoul of any other federal or state law. [ ]

Once a relator or the government has established the elements of a Stark Law violation, it becomes the defendant's burden to show that the indirect compensation arrangement exception shields it from liability. [ ]

* * *

III

We turn now to Tuomey's challenges to the judgment entered following the second trial. Tuomey asks for judgment as a matter of law because a reasonable jury could not have found that (1) the part-time employment contracts violated the Stark Law, or (2) Tuomey knowingly submitted false claims. Alternatively, Tuomey asks for a new trial because of the district court's refusal to tender certain jury instructions.

---

4   Because the Stark Law does not create its own right of action, the government in this case sought relief under the FCA, which provides a right of action with respect to false claims submitted for Medicare reimbursement.

* * *

1

Tuomey argues that it is entitled to judgment as a matter of law because the contracts between it and the physicians did not run afoul of the Stark Law. As we explain, however, a reasonable jury could find that Tuomey violated the Stark Law when it paid aggregate compensation to physicians that varied with or took into account the volume or value of actual or anticipated referrals to Tuomey.

To begin with, we note that the Stark Law's "volume or value" standard can be implicated when aggregate compensation varies with the volume or value of referrals, *or* otherwise takes into account the volume or value of referrals. [ ] That is precisely what the district court directed the jury in the second trial to assess. Tuomey insists, however, that our earlier opinion in this case foreclosed the jury's consideration of whether the contracts varied with the volume or value of referrals. Instead, says Tuomey, the *only* question that should have been put to the jury was "whether the contracts, on their face, took into account the value or volume of anticipated referrals." *Drakeford,* 675 F.3d at 409.

We disagree. The district court properly understood that the jury was entitled to pass on the contracts as they were actually implemented by the parties. We said as much in our earlier opinion, where

> we emphasize[d] that our holding . . . [was] limited to the issues we specifically address[ed]. On remand, a jury must determine, in light of our holding, whether the aggregate compensation received by the physicians under the contracts *varied with,* or took into account, the volume or value of the facility component referrals.

Id. at 409 n. 26 (emphasis added).

A reasonable jury could have found that Tuomey's contracts in fact compensated the physicians in a manner that varied with the volume or value of referrals. There are two different components of the physicians' compensation that we believe so varied. First, each year, the physicians were paid a base salary that was adjusted upward or downward depending on their collections from the prior year. In addition, the physicians received the bulk of their compensation in the form of a productivity bonus, pegged at eighty percent of the amount of their collections.

As Tuomey concedes, "the aggregate compensation received by the physicians under the Contracts was based solely on collections for personally performed professional services." [ ] And as we noted in our earlier opinion, there are referrals here, "consisting of the facility component of the physicians' personally performed services, and the resulting facility fee billed by Tuomey based upon that component." *Drakeford,* 675 F.3d at 407. In sum, the more procedures the physicians performed at the hospital, the more facility fees Tuomey collected, and the more compensation the physicians received in the form of increased base salaries and productivity bonuses.

The nature of this arrangement was confirmed by Tuomey's former Chief Financial Officer, William Paul Johnson, who admitted "that every time one of the 19 physicians . . . did a legitimate procedure on a Medicare patient at the hospital pursuant to the part-time agreement[,] the doctor [got] more money," and "the hospital also got more money." [ ] We thus think it plain that a reasonable jury could find that the physicians' compensation varied with the volume or value of actual referrals. The district court did not err in denying Tuomey's motion for judgment as a matter of law on this ground.[10]

2

Tuomey next argues that the district court erred in not granting its motion for judgment as a matter of law because it did not knowingly violate the FCA. Specifically, Tuomey claims that because it reasonably relied on the advice of counsel, no reasonable jury could find that Tuomey possessed the requisite intent to violate the FCA. Because the record here is replete with evidence indicating that Tuomey shopped for legal opinions approving of the employment contracts, while ignoring negative assessments, we disagree.

The FCA imposes civil liability on any person who "knowingly presents, or causes to be presented, a false or fraudulent claim for payment or approval" to an officer or employee of the United States Government. 31 U.S.C. § 3729(a)(1)(A), (b)(2)(A)(i). Under the Act, the term "knowingly" means that a person, with respect to information contained in a claim, (1) "has actual knowledge of the information;" (2) "acts in deliberate ignorance of the truth or falsity of the information;" or (3) "acts in reckless disregard of the truth or falsity of the information." *Id.* § 3729(b)(1). The purpose of

---

[10] We are not persuaded by Tuomey's reliance on commentary promulgated by the Centers for Medicare & Medicaid Services as it developed implementing regulations for the Stark Law. Tuomey points to a portion of the commentary wherein the agency states that the "fact that corresponding hospital services are billed would not invalidate an employed physician's personally performed work, for which the physician may be paid a productivity bonus (subject to the fair market value requirement)." 69 Fed. Reg. at 16089. But this statement deals only with a productivity bonus based on the fair market value of the work personally performed by a physician—it says nothing about the propriety of varying a physician's base salary based on the volume or value of referrals.

In any case, the commentary regarding productivity bonuses appears under a section of the regulations that specifically addresses comments related to the exception for bona fide employment relationships. This exception covers circumstances where there is a meaningful administrative relationship between the physician and the hospital. The jury was instructed on this exception at trial, and rejected it. Tuomey does not quarrel with that aspect of the jury's verdict; rather it contends that the commentary applies irrespective of whether a bona fide employment relationship actually exists. Nothing in the statute or the regulations, however, supports this notion.

the FCA's scienter requirement is to avoid punishing "honest mistakes or incorrect claims submitted through mere negligence." [ ]

The record evidence provides ample support for the jury's verdict as to Tuomey's intent. Indeed, McAnaney's testimony, summarized above, is alone sufficient to sweep aside Tuomey's claim of error.[11] We agree with the district court's conclusion that "a reasonable jury could have found that Tuomey possessed the requisite scienter once it determined to disregard McAnaney's remarks." [ ] A reasonable jury could indeed be troubled by Tuomey's seeming inaction in the face of McAnaney's warnings, particularly given Tuomey's aggressive efforts to avoid hearing precisely what McAnaney had to say regarding the contracts.

Nonetheless, a defendant may avoid liability under the FCA if it can show that it acted in good faith on the advice of counsel. *Cf. United States v. Painter,* 314 F.2d 939, 943 (4th Cir.1963) (holding, in a case involving fraud, that "[i]f in good faith reliance upon legal advice given him by a lawyer to whom he has made full disclosure of the facts, one engages in a course of conduct later found to be illegal, the trier of fact may in appropriate circumstances conclude the conduct was innocent because 'the guilty mind' was absent"). However, "consultation with a lawyer confers no automatic immunity from the legal consequences of conscious fraud." [ ] Rather, to establish the advice-of-counsel defense, the defendant must show the "(a) full disclosure of all pertinent facts to [counsel], and (b) good faith reliance on [counsel's] advice." [ ]

Tuomey contends that it provided full and accurate information regarding the proposed employment contracts to Hewson, who in turn advised Tuomey that the contracts did not run afoul of the Stark Law. But as the government aptly notes, "[i]n determining whether Tuomey reasonably relied on the advice of its counsel, the jury was entitled to consider *all* the advice given to it by *any* source."

In denying Tuomey's post-trial motions, the district court noted—and we agree—that a reasonable jury could have concluded that Tuomey was, after September 2005, no longer acting in good faith reliance on the advice of its counsel when it refused to give full consideration to McAnaney's negative assessment of the part-time employment contracts and terminated his representation. Tuomey defends its dismissal of McAnaney's warnings by claiming that his opinion was tainted by undue influence exerted by Drakeford and his counsel. But there was evidence before the jury suggesting that Tuomey also tried to procure a favorable opinion from McAnaney. Indeed, Tuomey's counsel admitted that he was trying "to steer McAnaney towards [Tuomey's] desired outcome" and that

---

[11] We note also that the jury at the second trial considered the deposition testimony of Tuomey executive Gregg Martin. While this evidence is (for reasons we have explained) not overly compelling in isolation, it is not without some value in showing that Tuomey was aware that its proposed contracts raised Stark Law concerns.

Tuomey needed to "continue playing along and influence the outcome of the game as best we can." [ ] Thus, a reasonable jury could conclude that Tuomey ignored McAnaney because it simply did not like what he had to say.

Tuomey points to the fact that it retained Steve Pratt, a prominent healthcare lawyer, and Richard Kusserow, former Inspector General at the United States Department of Health and Human Services, as further evidence that it acted in good faith and did not ignore McAnaney's warnings. Pratt rendered two opinions that generally approved of the employment contracts. But he did so without being told of McAnaney's unfavorable assessment, even though Tuomey had that information available to it at the time. In addition, Pratt reviewed and relied on the view of Tuomey's fair-market-value consultant that the employment contracts would compensate the physicians at fair market value, but he did not consider how the consultant arrived at its opinion. Nor did he know how much the doctors earned prior to entering into the contracts, or that the hospital stood to lose $1.5–2 million a year, not taking into account facility fees, by compensating the physicians above their collections. We thus think it entirely reasonable for a jury to look skeptically on Pratt's favorable advice regarding the contracts.

The same can be said of the Kusserow's advice. Kusserow—who was called by the government to rebut Tuomey's advice-of-counsel defense—advised Tuomey regarding the employment contracts about eighteen months before the parties retained McAnaney. As was the case with Pratt, he received no information regarding the fair market value of the employment contracts, information that Kusserow considered vital "to be able to do a full Stark analysis of [the proposed contracts]." [ ] And although Kusserow did say in a letter to Tuomey's counsel that he did not believe the contracts presented "significant Stark issues," [ ], he hedged considerably on that view because of "potentially troubling issues related to the productivity and [incentive bonus provisions in the contracts] that have not been fully addressed." [ ]

As the district court observed, "the jury evidently rejected Tuomey's advice of counsel defense" as of the date that Tuomey received McAnaney's warnings, "grounded on the fact that the jury excluded damages from [before the termination of McAnaney's engagement] in making its determination" of the civil penalty and damages. [ ] Thus, while Kusserow's advice was certainly relevant to Tuomey's advice-of-counsel defense, a reasonable jury could have determined that McAnaney's warnings (and Tuomey's subsequent inaction) were far more probative on the issue.

In sum, viewing the evidence in the light most favorable to the government, we have no cause to upset the jury's reasoned verdict that Tuomey violated the FCA.

IV

Finally, Tuomey makes several challenges to the $237,454,195 judgment entered against it. First, it argues that the district court improperly calculated the civil penalty. Next, it claims that the district court used the incorrect measure of actual damages. Finally, it brings constitutional challenges to the award under the Fifth and Eighth Amendments.

A defendant found liable under the FCA must pay the government "a civil penalty of" not less than $5,500 and not more than $11,000 "plus 3 times the amount of damages which the Government sustains because of that person." [ ] In this case, the jury found that Tuomey had submitted 21,730 false claims, for which it awarded actual damages of $39,313,065, which the district court trebled. The district court then added a civil penalty of $119,515,000 to that sum, which it calculated by multiplying the number of false claims by the $5,500 statutory minimum penalty.

* * *

1

According to Tuomey, the civil penalty assessed was improperly inflated because the jury was permitted to take into account both inpatient and outpatient procedures performed by the contracting physicians. Instead, relying on our earlier opinion in this case, Tuomey claims that the only relevant claims "were those Tuomey 'presented, or caused to be presented, to Medicare and Medicaid for payment of facility fees generated *as a result of outpatient procedures performed pursuant to the contracts.*'" [ ] Tuomey is incorrect.

It is true that the contracts solely addressed compensation for outpatient procedures. That is, the physicians' collections (which form the basis for both their base salaries and their productivity bonuses) do not account for the volume or value of inpatient procedures performed. Tuomey, however, takes out of context language from our earlier opinion recognizing this fact to suggest that we commanded that the relevant claims be limited to those seeking payment for outpatient procedures. We said nothing of the sort.

If a physician has a financial relationship with a hospital, then the Stark Law prohibits the physician from making *any* referral to that hospital for the furnishing of designated health services. *E.g., United States ex rel. Bartlett v. Ashcroft,* 39 F. Supp. 3d 656, 669 (W.D. Pa. 2014) ("Because a 'compensation arrangement' existed between Physician Defendants and [the] Hospital, the Stark [Law] prohibited Physician Defendants from making *any* patient referrals to [the] Hospital for designated health services." (emphasis added)). Inpatient hospital services are designated health services. [ ] And a referral includes "the request or establishment of a plan of care by a physician which includes the provision of the designated health service." [ ] Plainly, then, inpatient services constitute a prohibited referral for the furnishing of designated health services, and the district court properly instructed the jury to factor them into the damages calculation.

* * *

Finally, we do not discount the concerns raised by our concurring colleague regarding the result in this case. But having no found no cause to upset the jury's verdict in this case and no constitutional error, it is for Congress to consider whether changes to the Stark Law's reach are in order.

AFFIRMED.

WYNN, CIRCUIT JUDGE, concurring:

Because Tuomey opened the door to the admission of Kevin McAnaney's testimony by asserting an advice of counsel defense, and because I cannot say, based on the record before me, that no rational jury could have determined that Tuomey violated both the Stark Law and the False Claims Act, I concur in the outcome today.

But I write separately to emphasize the troubling picture this case paints: An impenetrably complex set of laws and regulations that will result in a likely death sentence for a community hospital in an already medically underserved area.

* * *

The government argues, among other things, that the McAnaney evidence went to the heart of an issue wholly beyond the scope of Rule 408's limited exclusionary ambit—namely, Tuomey's advice of counsel defense. With this, I must agree.

As explained by a district court in this Circuit in the context of a False Claims Act fraud claim, "good faith reliance on the advice of counsel may contradict any suggestion that a [defendant] 'knowingly' submitted a false claim." [ ] "[I]f a [defendant] seeks the advice of counsel in good faith, provides full and accurate information, receives advice which can be reasonably relied upon, and, in turn, faithfully follows that advice, it cannot be said that the defendant 'knowingly' submitted false information or acted with deliberate ignorance or reckless disregard of its falsity, even if that advice turns out in fact to be false." [ ] *United States v. Butler,* 211 F.3d 826, 833 (4th Cir.2000) (identifying the elements of the advice of counsel defense as "(a) full disclosure of all pertinent facts to [a lawyer], and (b) good faith reliance on the [lawyer]'s advice").

When a party raises an advice of counsel defense, however, all advice on the pertinent topic becomes fair game. "It has . . . become established that if a party interjects the 'advice of counsel' as an essential element of a claim or defense," then "all advice received concerning the same subject matter" is discoverable, not subject to protection by the attorney-client privilege, and, by logical extension, admissible at trial. [ ] . . . Having put the advice it got from its lawyers squarely at issue, Tuomey should not have been permitted to cherry-pick which advice of counsel the jury was permitted to hear. Instead, the jury should have been allowed to consider all the advice of all Tuomey's counsel—including McAnaney.

The record makes clear that . . . Tuomey did not follow McAnaney's advice. McAnaney advised Tuomey that the proposed contracts raised significant "red flags" under the Stark Law. [ ] McAnaney advised that Tuomey would have difficulty persuading the government that the contracts did not compensate the physicians in excess of fair market value. And McAnaney warned Tuomey that the contracts presented "an easy case to prosecute" for the government. [ ] Rather than heed this advice and back away from the contracts, however, Tuomey told McAnaney not to put his conclusions in writing and ended his engagement.

* * *

Given this complexity and the strict liability nature of the statute, a Stark Law "compliance program can help a physician or entity prove good faith and obtain leniency in the event of a violation; however, the Stark Law's complexity and frequent revisions make it difficult for physicians and entities to develop and implement such programs." [ ] Against this problematic backdrop, the availability of an advice of counsel defense should perhaps be especially robust in Stark Law cases prosecuted under the False Claims Act.

The False Claims Act discourages fraud against the federal government by imposing liability on "any person who . . . *knowingly* presents, or causes to be presented, a false or fraudulent claim for payment or approval." 31 U.S.C. § 3729(a)(1)(A) (emphasis added). The False Claims Act is meant "to indemnify the government . . . against losses caused by a defendant's *fraud*," [ ] as opposed to a defendant's mistake.

Accordingly, a defendant may skirt False Claims Act liability by showing good faith reliance on the advice of counsel. As the majority opinion recognizes, in fraud cases, " '[i]f in good faith reliance upon legal advice given him by a lawyer to whom he has made full disclosure of the facts, one engages in a course of conduct later found to be illegal,' " the trier of fact may conclude that the conduct was innocent because " 'the guilty mind' was absent." [ ]

In the context of the Stark Law, it is easy to see how even diligent counsel could wind up giving clients incorrect advice. Between the law's being amended to have a broader scope but then narrowed with various exceptions, along with the promulgation and amendment of copious associated rules and regulations, "the Stark Law bec[ame] a classic example of a moving target. For lawyers, who must depend on the predictability of the law when they give counsel to their clients, such unpredictability [i]s an unusually heavy burden." [ ]

* * *

Nevertheless, as the majority opinion notes, "a reasonable jury could have concluded that Tuomey was . . . no longer acting in good faith reliance on the advice of its counsel when it refused to give full consideration to McAnaney's negative assessment of the" contracts. [ ] As already explained, McAnaney, the former Chief of the Industry Guidance Branch at the Department of Health and Human Services' Office of Counsel to the Inspector General, also served as Tuomey's counsel. And he advised Tuomey that the proposed arrangements raised significant red flags and may well be unlawful. Had Tuomey followed McAnaney's advice, it likely would have faced no lawsuit in which to raise an advice of counsel, or any other, defense.

This case is troubling. It seems as if, even for well-intentioned health care providers, the Stark Law has become a booby trap rigged with strict liability and potentially ruinous exposure—especially when coupled with the False Claims Act. Yet, the district court did not abuse its discretion when it granted a new trial and the jury did not act irrationally when it determined that Tuomey violated both the Stark Law and the False Claims Act. Accordingly, I must concur in the outcome reached by the majority.

NOTES AND QUESTIONS

1. As in-house counsel for a health system about to undertake an arrangement with doctors that might implicate Stark, what advice would you give regarding soliciting the opinion of outside counsel?

2. The $237 million verdict affirmed by the Fourth Circuit exceeded the annual revenues of the Tuomey Healthcare System. Defendant entered into a settlement of its ten-year legal battle pursuant to which it would pay the government $72.4 million and would sell the system to Palmetto Health, a Columbia, South Carolina system with which it had previously indicated it would partner. Dr. Drakeford, the whistleblower who declined to enter into the challenged agreement received $18.1 million from the settlement. See Lisa Schenker, Tuomey Will Pay U.S. $72.4 Million to Duck $237 Million False Claims Verdict, Mod. Healthcare (Oct. 16, 2015). What is your verdict on *Tuomey*? Object lesson about the flaws inherent in the Stark law? Important message to those who would flaunt the law?

Add at page 1156 at the end of the first carryover paragraph:

On February 12, 2016, CMS released its final rule detailing, and to some extent relaxing, the responsibilities of providers and suppliers to report and return overpayments pursuant to the 60-day rule discussed in the text. Dept. of Health & Human Servs. Medicare Program; Reporting and Returning of Overpayments, 81 Fed. Reg. 7654 (February 12, 2016). The new guidance provides that an overpayment has not been "identified" until a provider has quantified the overpayment or should have done so by exercising "reasonable diligence." Thus the sixty-day clock does not start running until a provider that has discovered an overpayment has determined (or should have determined) the amount of overpayments received. However, CMS was careful to make clear that it was not endorsing an endless pursuit of every detail of overpayment: it indicated that reasonable diligence should, absent extraordinary circumstances, not exceed six months. Notably, a district court in the Second Circuit had held that the obligation to report and repay began sixty days after a provider was first put on notice of overpayment where hospitals had dragged their feet in taking steps to quantify the extent of erroneous overpayments from the Medicaid program. Kane ex rel. U.S. v. Healthfirst, Inc., 120 F. Supp. 3d 370 (S.D.N.Y. 2015). The rule also provides that the 60-day rule applies only to overpayments identified within 6 years after received, not the 10-year lookback period originally proposed.

CHAPTER 14

ANTITRUST

■ ■ ■

II. CARTELS AND PROFESSIONALISM

B. COLLECTIVE ACTIVITIES WITH JUSTIFICATIONS

1. Restrictions on Advertising and Dissemination of Information

Add at page 1191 before *Note: Physician Staff Privileges*:

NORTH CAROLINA STATE BOARD OF DENTAL EXAMINERS V. FEDERAL TRADE COMMISSION

Supreme Court of the United States, 2015.
135 S.Ct. 1101.

KENNEDY, J., delivered the opinion of the Court, in which ROBERTS, C.J., and GINSBURG, BREYER, SOTOMAYOR, and KAGAN, JJ., joined. ALITO, J., filed a dissenting opinion, in which SCALIA and THOMAS, JJ., joined.

JUSTICE KENNEDY delivered the opinion of the Court.

This case arises from an antitrust challenge to the actions of a state regulatory board. A majority of the board's members are engaged in the active practice of the profession it regulates. The question is whether the board's actions are protected from Sherman Act regulation under the doctrine of state-action antitrust immunity, as defined and applied in this Court's decisions beginning with *Parker v. Brown,* 317 U.S. 341, 63 S.Ct. 307, 87 L.Ed. 315 (1943).

I

A

In its Dental Practice Act (Act), North Carolina has declared the practice of dentistry to be a matter of public concern requiring regulation. . . . Under the Act, the North Carolina State Board of Dental Examiners (Board) is "the agency of the State for the regulation of the practice of dentistry." [ ]

The Board's principal duty is to create, administer, and enforce a licensing system for dentists. [ ] To perform that function it has broad authority over licensees. [ ] The Board's authority with respect to

109

unlicensed persons, however, is more restricted: like "any resident citizen," the Board may file suit to "perpetually enjoin any person from . . . unlawfully practicing dentistry." [ ]

The Act provides that six of the Board's eight members must be licensed dentists engaged in the active practice of dentistry. [ ] They are elected by other licensed dentists in North Carolina, who cast their ballots in elections conducted by the Board. [ ] The seventh member must be a licensed and practicing dental hygienist, and he or she is elected by other licensed hygienists. [ ] The final member is referred to by the Act as a "consumer" and is appointed by the Governor. [ ] All members serve 3-year terms, and no person may serve more than two consecutive terms. [ ] The Act does not create any mechanism for the removal of an elected member of the Board by a public official.

* * *

B

In the 1990's, dentists in North Carolina started whitening teeth. Many of those who did so, including 8 of the Board's 10 members during the period at issue in this case, earned substantial fees for that service. By 2003, nondentists arrived on the scene. They charged lower prices for their services than the dentists did. Dentists soon began to complain to the Board about their new competitors. Few complaints warned of possible harm to consumers. Most expressed a principal concern with the low prices charged by nondentists.

Responding to these filings, the Board opened an investigation into nondentist teeth whitening. A dentist member was placed in charge of the inquiry. Neither the Board's hygienist member nor its consumer member participated in this undertaking. The Board's chief operations officer remarked that the Board was "going forth to do battle" with nondentists. [ ] The Board's concern did not result in a formal rule or regulation reviewable by the independent Rules Review Commission, even though the Act does not, by its terms, specify that teeth whitening is "the practice of dentistry."

Starting in 2006, the Board issued at least 47 cease-and-desist letters on its official letterhead to nondentist teeth whitening service providers and product manufacturers. Many of those letters directed the recipient to cease "all activity constituting the practice of dentistry"; warned that the unlicensed practice of dentistry is a crime; and strongly implied (or expressly stated) that teeth whitening constitutes "the practice of dentistry." [ ] In early 2007, the Board persuaded the North Carolina Board of Cosmetic Art Examiners to warn cosmetologists against providing teeth whitening services. Later that year, the Board sent letters to mall operators, stating that kiosk teeth whiteners were violating the Dental

Practice Act and advising that the malls consider expelling violators from their premises.

These actions had the intended result. Nondentists ceased offering teeth whitening services in North Carolina.

C

In 2010, the Federal Trade Commission (FTC) filed an administrative complaint charging the Board with violating § 5 of the Federal Trade Commission Act. [ ] The FTC alleged that the Board's concerted action to exclude nondentists from the market for teeth whitening services in North Carolina constituted an anticompetitive and unfair method of competition.

* * *

Following other proceedings not relevant here, the ALJ conducted a hearing on the merits and determined the Board had unreasonably restrained trade in violation of antitrust law. On appeal, the FTC again sustained the ALJ. The FTC rejected the Board's public safety justification, noting, *inter alia,* "a wealth of evidence . . . suggesting that non-dentist provided teeth whitening is a safe cosmetic procedure." [ ]

The FTC ordered the Board to stop sending the cease-and-desist letters or other communications that stated nondentists may not offer teeth whitening services and products. It further ordered the Board to issue notices to all earlier recipients of the Board's cease-and-desist orders advising them of the Board's proper sphere of authority and saying, among other options, that the notice recipients had a right to seek declaratory rulings in state court.

On petition for review, the Court of Appeals for the Fourth Circuit affirmed the FTC in all respects. [ ] This Court granted certiorari. [ ]

II

Federal antitrust law is a central safeguard for the Nation's free market structures. In this regard it is "as important to the preservation of economic freedom and our free-enterprise system as the Bill of Rights is to the protection of our fundamental personal freedoms." [ ] The antitrust laws declare a considered and decisive prohibition by the Federal Government of cartels, price fixing, and other combinations or practices that undermine the free market.

The Sherman Act . . . serves to promote robust competition, which in turn empowers the States and provides their citizens with opportunities to pursue their own and the public's welfare. See *FTC v. Ticor Title Ins. Co.,* 504 U.S. 621, 632, 112 S.Ct. 2169, 119 L.Ed.2d 410 (1992). The States, however, when acting in their respective realm, need not adhere in all contexts to a model of unfettered competition. While "the States regulate their economies in many ways not inconsistent with the antitrust laws," [ ] in some spheres they impose restrictions on occupations, confer exclusive or shared rights to dominate a market, or otherwise limit competition to achieve public objectives. If every duly enacted state law or policy were required to conform to the mandates of the Sherman Act, thus promoting competition at the expense of other values a State may deem fundamental, federal antitrust law would impose an impermissible burden on the States' power to regulate. [ ]

For these reasons, the Court in *Parker v. Brown* interpreted the antitrust laws to confer immunity on anticompetitive conduct by the States when acting in their sovereign capacity. [ ] That ruling recognized Congress' purpose to respect the federal balance and to "embody in the Sherman Act the federalism principle that the States possess a significant measure of sovereignty under our Constitution." * * *

III

In this case the Board argues its members were invested by North Carolina with the power of the State and that, as a result, the Board's actions are cloaked with *Parker* immunity. This argument fails, however. A nonsovereign actor controlled by active market participants—such as the Board—enjoys *Parker* immunity only if it satisfies two requirements: "first that 'the challenged restraint ... be one clearly articulated and affirmatively expressed as state policy,' and second that 'the policy . . . be actively supervised by the State.' " *FTC v. Phoebe Putney Health System, Inc.,* 568 U.S. ___, ___, 133 S.Ct. 1003, 1010, 185 L.Ed.2d 43 (2013) (quoting *California Retail Liquor Dealers Assn. v. Midcal Aluminum, Inc.,* 445 U.S. 97, 105, 100 S.Ct. 937, 63 L.Ed.2d 233 (1980)). The parties have assumed that the clear articulation requirement is satisfied, and we do the same. While North Carolina prohibits the unauthorized practice of dentistry, however, its Act is silent on whether that broad prohibition covers teeth whitening. Here, the Board did not receive active supervision by the State when it interpreted the Act as addressing teeth whitening and when it enforced that policy by issuing cease-and-desist letters to nondentist teeth whiteners.

A

Although state-action immunity exists to avoid conflicts between state sovereignty and the Nation's commitment to a policy of robust competition, *Parker* immunity is not unbounded. "[G]iven the fundamental national values of free enterprise and economic competition that are embodied in the federal antitrust laws, 'state action immunity is disfavored, much as are repeals by implication.' " [ ]

An entity may not invoke *Parker* immunity unless the actions in question are an exercise of the State's sovereign power. [ ] State legislation and "decision[s] of a state supreme court, acting legislatively rather than judicially," will satisfy this standard, and "*ipso facto* are exempt from the operation of the antitrust laws" because they are an undoubted exercise of state sovereign authority. [ ]

But while the Sherman Act confers immunity on the States' own anticompetitive policies out of respect for federalism, it does not always confer immunity where, as here, a State delegates control over a market to a non-sovereign actor. See *Parker, supra,* at 351, 63 S.Ct. 307 ("[A] state does not give immunity to those who violate the Sherman Act by authorizing them to violate it, or by declaring that their action is lawful"). For purposes of *Parker,* a nonsovereign actor is one whose conduct does not automatically qualify as that of the sovereign State itself. [ ] State agencies are not simply by their governmental character sovereign actors for purposes of state-action immunity. See *Goldfarb v. Virginia State Bar,* 421 U.S. 773, 791, 95 S.Ct. 2004, 44 L.Ed.2d 572 (1975) ("The fact that the State Bar is a state agency for some limited purposes does not create an antitrust shield that allows it to foster anticompetitive practices for the benefit of its members"). Immunity for state agencies, therefore, requires more than a mere facade of state involvement, for it is necessary in light of *Parker* 's rationale to ensure the States accept political accountability for anticompetitive conduct they permit and control. [ ]

Limits on state-action immunity are most essential when the State seeks to delegate its regulatory power to active market participants, for established ethical standards may blend with private anticompetitive motives in a way difficult even for market participants to discern. Dual allegiances are not always apparent to an actor. In consequence, active market participants cannot be allowed to regulate their own markets free from antitrust accountability. See *Midcal, supra,* at 106, 100 S.Ct. 937 ("The national policy in favor of competition cannot be thwarted by casting [a] gauzy cloak of state involvement over what is essentially a private price-fixing arrangement"). Indeed, prohibitions against anticompetitive self-regulation by active market participants are an axiom of federal antitrust policy. * * * So it follows that, under *Parker* and the Supremacy Clause, the States' greater power to attain an end does not include the lesser power to negate the congressional judgment embodied in the Sherman Act through unsupervised delegations to active market participants.

Parker immunity requires that the anticompetitive conduct of nonsovereign actors, especially those authorized by the State to regulate their own profession, result from procedures that suffice to make it the State's own. See *Goldfarb, supra,* at 790, 95 S.Ct. 2004; see also 1A P. Areeda & H. Hovencamp, Antitrust Law ¶ 226, p. 180 (4th ed. 2013) (Areeda & Hovencamp). The question is not whether the challenged conduct is efficient, well-functioning, or wise. See *Ticor, supra,* at 634–635, 112 S.Ct. 2169. Rather, it is "whether anticompetitive conduct engaged in by [nonsovereign actors] should be deemed state action and thus shielded from the antitrust laws." *Patrick v. Burget,* 486 U.S. 94, 100, 108 S.Ct. 1658, 100 L.Ed.2d 83 (1988).

To answer this question, the Court applies the two-part test set forth in *California Retail Liquor Dealers Assn. v. Midcal Aluminum, Inc.,* 445 U.S. 97, 100 S.Ct. 937, 63 L.Ed.2d 233, a case arising from California's delegation of price-fixing authority to wine merchants. Under *Midcal,* "[a] state law or regulatory scheme cannot be the basis for antitrust immunity unless, first, the State has articulated a clear policy to allow the anticompetitive conduct, and second, the State provides active supervision of [the] anticompetitive conduct." [ ]

Midcal's clear articulation requirement is satisfied "where the displacement of competition [is] the inherent, logical, or ordinary result of the exercise of authority delegated by the state legislature. In that scenario, the State must have foreseen and implicitly endorsed the anticompetitive effects as consistent with its policy goals." *Phoebe Putney,* 568 U.S., at ___, 133 S.Ct., at 1013. The active supervision requirement demands, *inter alia,* "that state officials have and exercise power to review particular anticompetitive acts of private parties and disapprove those that fail to accord with state policy." [ ]

The two requirements set forth in *Midcal* provide a proper analytical framework to resolve the ultimate question whether an anticompetitive policy is indeed the policy of a State. The first requirement—clear articulation—rarely will achieve that goal by itself, for a policy may satisfy this test yet still be defined at so high a level of generality as to leave open critical questions about how and to what extent the market should be regulated. [ ] Entities purporting to act under state authority might diverge from the State's considered definition of the public good. The resulting asymmetry between a state policy and its implementation can invite private self-dealing. The second *Midcal* requirement—active supervision— seeks to avoid this harm by requiring the State to review and approve interstitial policies made by the entity claiming immunity.

Midcal's supervision rule "stems from the recognition that '[w]here a private party is engaging in anticompetitive activity, there is a real danger that he is acting to further his own interests, rather than the governmental interests of the State.'" [ ] Concern about the private incentives of active market participants animates *Midcal*'s supervision mandate, which demands "realistic assurance that a private party's anticompetitive conduct promotes state policy, rather than merely the party's individual interests." [ ]

B

In determining whether anticompetitive policies and conduct are indeed the action of a State in its sovereign capacity, there are instances in which an actor can be excused from *Midcal*'s active supervision requirement. In *Hallie v. Eau Claire,* 471 U.S. 34, 45, 105 S.Ct. 1713, 85 L.Ed.2d 24 (1985), the Court held municipalities are subject exclusively to *Midcal*'s "clear articulation" requirement. That rule, the Court observed, is consistent with the objective of ensuring that the policy at issue be one enacted by the State itself. *Hallie* explained that "[w]here the actor is a municipality, there is little or no danger that it is involved in a private price-fixing arrangement. The only real danger is that it will seek to further purely parochial public interests at the expense of more overriding state goals." 471 U.S., at 47, 105 S.Ct. 1713. *Hallie* further observed that municipalities are electorally accountable and lack the kind of private incentives characteristic of active participants in the market. [ ] Critically, the municipality in *Hallie* exercised a wide range of governmental powers across different economic spheres, substantially reducing the risk that it would pursue private interests while regulating any single field. [ ] That *Hallie* excused municipalities from *Midcal*'s supervision rule for these reasons all but confirms the rule's applicability to actors controlled by active market participants, who ordinarily have none of the features justifying the narrow exception *Hallie* identified.

* * *

In *Ticor* the Court affirmed that *Midcal*'s limits on delegation must ensure that "[a]ctual state involvement, not deference to private price-fixing arrangements under the general auspices of state law, is the precondition for immunity from federal law." 504 U.S., at 633, 112 S.Ct. 2169. And in *Phoebe Putney* the Court observed that *Midcal*'s active supervision requirement, in particular, is an essential condition of state-action immunity when a nonsovereign actor has "an incentive to pursue [its] own self-interest under the guise of implementing state policies." [ ] The lesson is clear: *Midcal*'s active supervision test is an essential prerequisite of *Parker* immunity for any nonsovereign entity—public or private—controlled by active market participants.

C

The Board argues entities designated by the States as agencies are exempt from *Midcal*'s second requirement. That premise, however, cannot be reconciled with the Court's repeated conclusion that the need for supervision turns not on the formal designation given by States to regulators but on the risk that active market participants will pursue private interests in restraining trade.

State agencies controlled by active market participants, who possess singularly strong private interests, pose the very risk of self-dealing *Midcal*'s supervision requirement was created to address. [ ] This conclusion does not question the good faith of state officers but rather is an assessment of the structural risk of market participants' confusing their own interests with the State's policy goals. [ ]

The Court applied this reasoning to a state agency in *Goldfarb*. There the Court denied immunity to a state agency (the Virginia State Bar) controlled by market participants (lawyers) because the agency had "joined in what is essentially a private anticompetitive activity" for "the benefit of its members." [ ] This emphasis on the Bar's private interests explains why *Goldfarb*, though it predates *Midcal*, considered the lack of supervision by the Virginia Supreme Court to be a principal reason for denying immunity. [ ]

While *Hallie* stated "it is likely that active state supervision would also not be required" for agencies, [ ] the entity there, as was later the case in *Omni*, was an electorally accountable municipality with general regulatory powers and no private price-fixing agenda. In that and other respects the municipality was more like prototypical state agencies, not specialized boards dominated by active market participants. In important regards, agencies controlled by market participants are more similar to private trade associations vested by States with regulatory authority than to the agencies *Hallie* considered. And as the Court observed three years after *Hallie*, "[t]here is no doubt that the members of such associations often have economic incentives to restrain competition and that the product standards set by such associations have a serious potential for anticompetitive harm." *Allied Tube*, 486 U.S., at 500, 108 S.Ct. 1931. For that reason, those associations must satisfy *Midcal*'s active supervision standard. See *Midcal*, 445 U.S., at 105–106, 100 S.Ct. 937.

The similarities between agencies controlled by active market participants and private trade associations are not eliminated simply because the former are given a formal designation by the State, vested with a measure of government power, and required to follow some procedural rules. * * * When a State empowers a group of active market participants to decide who can participate in its market, and on what terms, the need for supervision is manifest. [ ] The Court holds today that a state board on which a controlling number of decisionmakers are active market participants in the occupation the board regulates must satisfy *Midcal*'s active supervision requirement in order to invoke state-action antitrust immunity. For that reason, those associations must satisfy *Midcal*'s active supervision standard.

D

The State argues that allowing this FTC order to stand will discourage dedicated citizens from serving on state agencies that regulate their own occupation. If this were so—and, for reasons to be noted, it need not be so—there would be some cause for concern. The States have a sovereign interest in structuring their governments, [ ] and may conclude there are substantial benefits to staffing their agencies with experts in complex and technical subjects. [ ] There is, moreover, a long tradition of citizens esteemed by their professional colleagues devoting time, energy, and talent to enhancing the dignity of their calling.

* * *

. . . The Board argues, however, that the potential for money damages will discourage members of regulated occupations from participating in state government. . . . But this case, which does not present a claim for money damages, does not offer occasion to address the question whether agency officials, including board members, may, under some circumstances, enjoy immunity from damages liability. [ ] And, of course, the States may provide for the defense and indemnification of agency members in the event of litigation.

States, furthermore, can ensure *Parker* immunity is available to agencies by adopting clear policies to displace competition; and, if agencies controlled by active market participants interpret or enforce those policies, the States may provide active supervision. Precedent confirms this principle. The Court has rejected the argument that it would be unwise to apply the antitrust laws to professional regulation absent compliance with the prerequisites for invoking *Parker* immunity:

> "[Respondents] contend that effective peer review is essential to the provision of quality medical care and that any threat of antitrust liability will prevent physicians from participating openly and actively in peer-review proceedings. This argument, however, essentially challenges the wisdom of applying the antitrust laws to the sphere of medical care, and as such is properly directed to the legislative branch. To the extent that Congress has declined to exempt medical peer review from the reach of the antitrust laws, peer review is immune from antitrust scrutiny only if the State effectively has made this conduct its own." *Patrick,* 486 U.S. at 105–106, 108 S.Ct. 1658 (footnote omitted).

The reasoning of *Patrick v. Burget* applies to this case with full force, particularly in light of the risks licensing boards dominated by market participants may pose to the free market. . . .

E

The Board does not contend in this Court that its anticompetitive conduct was actively supervised by the State or that it should receive *Parker* immunity on that basis.

By statute, North Carolina delegates control over the practice of dentistry to the Board. The Act, however, says nothing about teeth whitening, a practice that did not exist when it was passed. . . . Whether or not the Board exceeded its powers under North Carolina law, [ ] there is no evidence here of any decision by the State to initiate or concur with the Board's actions against the nondentists.

IV

The Board does not claim that the State exercised active, or indeed any, supervision over its conduct regarding nondentist teeth whiteners; and, as a result, no specific supervisory systems can be reviewed here. It suffices to note that the inquiry regarding active supervision is flexible and context-dependent. Active supervision need not entail day-to-day involvement in an agency's operations or micromanagement of its every decision. Rather, the question is whether the State's review mechanisms provide "realistic assurance" that a nonsovereign actor's anticompetitive conduct "promotes state policy, rather than merely the party's individual interests." [ ]

The Court has identified only a few constant requirements of active supervision: The supervisor must review the substance of the anticompetitive decision, not merely the procedures followed to produce it, see *Patrick,* 486 U.S., at 102–103, 108 S.Ct. 1658; the supervisor must have the power to veto or modify particular decisions to ensure they accord with state policy, see *ibid.*; and the "mere potential for state supervision is not an adequate substitute for a decision by the State," *Ticor, supra,* at 638, 112 S.Ct. 2169. Further, the state supervisor may not itself be an active market participant. In general, however, the adequacy of supervision otherwise will depend on all the circumstances of a case.

* * *

The Sherman Act protects competition while also respecting federalism. It does not authorize the States to abandon markets to the unsupervised control of active market participants, whether trade associations or hybrid agencies. If a State wants to rely on active market participants as regulators, it must provide active supervision if state-action immunity under *Parker* is to be invoked.

The judgment of the Court of Appeals for the Fourth Circuit is affirmed.

It is so ordered.

JUSTICE ALITO, with whom JUSTICE SCALIA and JUSTICE THOMAS join, dissenting.

The Court's decision in this case is based on a serious misunderstanding of the doctrine of state-action antitrust immunity that this Court recognized more than 60 years ago in *Parker v. Brown,* 317 U.S. 341, 63 S.Ct. 307, 87 L.Ed. 315 (1943). In *Parker,* the Court held that the Sherman Act does not prevent the States from continuing their age-old practice of enacting measures, such as licensing requirements, that are designed to protect the public health and welfare. *Id.*, at 352, 63 S.Ct. 307. The case now before us involves precisely this type of state regulation— North Carolina's laws governing the practice of dentistry, which are administered by the North Carolina Board of Dental Examiners (Board).

Today, however, the Court takes the unprecedented step of holding that *Parker* does not apply to the North Carolina Board because the Board is not structured in a way that merits a good-government seal of approval; that is, it is made up of practicing dentists who have a financial incentive to use the licensing laws to further the financial interests of the State's dentists. There is nothing new about the structure of the North Carolina Board. When the States first created medical and dental boards, well before the Sherman Act was enacted, they began to staff them in this way. Nor is there anything new about the suspicion that the North Carolina Board— in attempting to prevent persons other than dentists from performing teeth-whitening procedures—was serving the interests of dentists and not the public. Professional and occupational licensing requirements have often been used in such a way. But that is not what *Parker* immunity is about. Indeed, the very state program involved in that case was unquestionably designed to benefit the regulated entities, California raisin growers.

The question before us is not whether such programs serve the public interest. The question, instead, is whether this case is controlled by *Parker,* and the answer to that question is clear. Under *Parker,* the Sherman Act and the Federal Trade Commission Act [ ] do not apply to state agencies; the North Carolina Board of Dental Examiners is a state agency; and that is the end of the matter. By straying from this simple path, the Court has not only distorted *Parker*; it has headed into a morass. Determining whether a state agency is structured in a way that militates against regulatory capture is no easy task, and there is reason to fear that today's decision will spawn confusion. The Court has veered off course, and therefore I cannot go along.

I

* * *

The Court's holding in *Parker* was not based on either the language of the Sherman Act or anything in the legislative history affirmatively showing that the Act was not meant to apply to the States. Instead, the Court reasoned that "[i]n a dual system of government in which, under the Constitution, the states are sovereign, save only as Congress may constitutionally subtract from their authority, an unexpressed purpose to nullify a state's control over its officers and agents is not lightly to be attributed to Congress." 317 U.S., at 351, 63 S.Ct. 307. For the Congress that enacted the Sherman Act in 1890, it would have been a truly radical and almost certainly futile step to attempt to prevent the States from exercising their traditional regulatory authority, and the *Parker* Court refused to assume that the Act was meant to have such an effect.

When the basis for the *Parker* state-action doctrine is understood, the Court's error in this case is plain. In 1890, the regulation of the practice of medicine and dentistry was regarded as falling squarely within the States' sovereign police power. By that time, many States had established medical and dental boards, often staffed by doctors or dentists, and had given those boards the authority to confer and revoke licenses. * * * Thus, the North Carolina statutes establishing and specifying the powers of the State Board of Dental Examiners represent precisely the kind of state regulation that the *Parker* exemption was meant to immunize.

II

As noted above, the only question in this case is whether the North Carolina Board of Dental Examiners is really a state agency, and the answer to that question is clearly yes.

* * *

The Board is not a private or "nonsovereign" entity that the State of North Carolina has attempted to immunize from federal antitrust scrutiny. *Parker* made it clear that a State may not " 'give immunity to those who violate the Sherman Act by authorizing them to violate it, or by declaring that their action is lawful.' " [ ] When the *Parker* Court disapproved of any such attempt, it cited *Northern Securities Co. v. United States,* 193 U.S. 197, 24 S.Ct. 436, 48 L.Ed. 679 (1904), to show what it had in mind. In that case, the Court held that a State's act of chartering a corporation did not shield the corporation's monopolizing activities from federal antitrust law. *Id.,* at 344–345, 63 S.Ct. 307. Nothing similar is involved here. North Carolina did not authorize a private entity to enter into an anticompetitive arrangement; rather, North Carolina *created a state agency* and gave that agency the power to regulate a particular subject affecting public health and safety.

Nothing in *Parker* supports the type of inquiry that the Court now prescribes. The Court crafts a test under which state agencies that are "controlled by active market participants," [ ] must demonstrate active state supervision in order to be immune from federal antitrust law. The Court thus treats these state agencies like private entities. But in *Parker,* the Court did not examine the structure of the California program to determine if it had been captured by private interests. If the Court had done so, the case would certainly have come out differently, because California conditioned its regulatory measures on the participation and approval of market actors in the relevant industry.

* * *

III

The Court goes astray because it forgets the origin of the *Parker* doctrine and is misdirected by subsequent cases that extended that doctrine (in certain circumstances) to private entities. The Court requires the North Carolina Board to satisfy the two-part test set out in *California Retail Liquor Dealers Assn. v. Midcal Aluminum, Inc.,* 445 U.S. 97, 100 S.Ct. 937, 63 L.Ed.2d 233 (1980), but the party claiming *Parker* immunity in that case was not a state agency but a private trade association. Such an entity is entitled to *Parker* immunity, *Midcal* held, only if the anticompetitive conduct at issue was both " 'clearly articulated' " and " 'actively supervised by the State itself.' " [ ] Those requirements are needed where a State authorizes private parties to engage in anticompetitive conduct. They serve to identify those situations in which conduct *by private parties* can be regarded as the conduct of a State. But when the conduct in question is the conduct of a state agency, no such inquiry is required.

This case falls into the latter category, and therefore *Midcal* is inapposite. The North Carolina Board is not a private trade association. It is a state agency, created and empowered by the State to regulate an industry affecting public health. It would not exist if the State had not created it. And for purposes of *Parker,* its membership is irrelevant; what matters is that it is part of the government of the sovereign State of North Carolina.

Our decision in *Hallie v. Eau Claire,* 471 U.S. 34, 105 S.Ct. 1713, 85 L.Ed.2d 24 (1985), which involved Sherman Act claims against a municipality, not a State agency, is similarly inapplicable. In *Hallie,* the plaintiff argued that the two-pronged *Midcal* test should be applied, but the Court disagreed. The Court acknowledged that municipalities "are not themselves sovereign." [ ] But recognizing that a municipality is "an arm of the State," [ ] the Court held that a municipality should be required to satisfy only the first prong of the *Midcal* test (requiring a clearly articulated state policy). [ ] That municipalities are not sovereign was critical to our analysis in *Hallie,* and thus that decision has no application in a case, like this one, involving a state agency.

Here, however, the Court not only disregards the North Carolina Board's status as a full-fledged state agency; it treats the Board less favorably than a municipality. This is puzzling. States are sovereign. * * *

The Court recognizes that municipalities, although not sovereign, nevertheless benefit from a more lenient standard for state-action immunity than private entities. Yet under the Court's approach, the North Carolina Board of Dental Examiners, a full-fledged state agency, is treated like a private actor and must demonstrate that the State actively supervises its actions.

IV

Not only is the Court's decision inconsistent with the underlying theory of *Parker*; it will create practical problems and is likely to have far-reaching effects on the States' regulation of professions. As previously noted, state medical and dental boards have been staffed by practitioners since they were first created, and there are obvious advantages to this approach. It is reasonable for States to decide that the individuals best able to regulate technical professions are practitioners with expertise in those very professions. Staffing the State Board of Dental Examiners with certified public accountants would certainly lessen the risk of actions that place the well-being of dentists over those of the public, but this would also compromise the State's interest in sensibly regulating a technical profession in which lay people have little expertise.

As a result of today's decision, States may find it necessary to change the composition of medical, dental, and other boards, but it is not clear what sort of changes are needed to satisfy the test that the Court now adopts. The Court faults the structure of the North Carolina Board because "active market participants" constitute "a controlling number of [the] decisionmakers," [ ] but this test raises many questions.

What is a "controlling number"? Is it a majority? And if so, why does the Court eschew that term? Or does the Court mean to leave open the possibility that something less than a majority might suffice in particular circumstances? Suppose that active market participants constitute a voting bloc that is generally able to get its way? How about an obstructionist minority or an agency chair empowered to set the agenda or veto regulations?

Who is an "active market participant"? If Board members withdraw from practice during a short term of service but typically return to practice when their terms end, does that mean that they are not active market participants during their period of service?

What is the scope of the market in which a member may not participate while serving on the board? Must the market be relevant to the particular regulation being challenged or merely to the jurisdiction of the entire agency? Would the result in the present case be different if a majority of the Board members, though practicing dentists, did not provide teeth whitening services? What if they were orthodontists, periodontists, and the like? And how much participation makes a person "active" in the market?

The answers to these questions are not obvious, but the States must predict the answers in order to make informed choices about how to constitute their agencies.

I suppose that all this will be worked out by the lower courts and the Federal Trade Commission (FTC), but the Court's approach raises a more fundamental question, and that is why the Court's inquiry should stop with an examination of the structure of a state licensing board. When the Court asks whether market participants control the North Carolina Board, the Court in essence is asking whether this regulatory body has been captured by the entities that it is supposed to regulate. Regulatory capture can occur in many ways. So why ask only whether the members of a board are active market participants? The answer may be that determining when regulatory capture has occurred is no simple task. That answer provides a reason for relieving courts from the obligation to make such determinations at all. It does not explain why it is appropriate for the Court to adopt the rather crude test for capture that constitutes the holding of today's decision.

V

The Court has created a new standard for distinguishing between private and state actors for purposes of federal antitrust immunity. This new standard is not true to the *Parker* doctrine; it diminishes our traditional respect for federalism and state sovereignty; and it will be difficult to apply. I therefore respectfully dissent.

NOTES

1. The significant implications of this case for state medical and professional licensure are discussed in Chapter 2 of this Supplement.

2. In one of the first applications of the *North Carolina Dental* case, Teladoc Inc. v. Texas Medical Board, 112 F. Supp. 3d 529 (W.D. Tex 2015), a district court analyzed a rule of a state medical board that required a face-to-face visit before a physician can issue a prescription to a patient, regardless of medical necessity. Plaintiff's antitrust claim asserted that the Texas board, which regulates the practice of medicine and was comprised of active members of the medical profession, restrained the ability of telemedicine practitioners to compete and reduced patient access to affordable care. The court held that in order to satisfy the affirmative defense of state action the state must both have the power to veto or modify decisions to ensure they accord with state policy; and review the substance of the board's decision. The fact that board decisions were subject to judicial review did not satisfy the active supervision requirement because courts cannot review the substantive policies at issue or modify the board's actions.

III. HEALTH CARE ENTERPRISES,
INTEGRATION AND FINANCING

D. MERGERS AND ACQUISITIONS

1. Hospital Mergers

Add at page 1262 at the end of Note 3:

Although the FTC prevailed in the Sixth Circuit which upheld the lower court's decision in ProMedica Health System v. FTC, 749 F.3d 559 (6th Cir. 2014), the government's winning streak in hospital mergers came to an end as two district courts refused to grant preliminary injunctions in hospital merger challenges. FTC v. Penn State Hershey Medical Center, No. 1:15-CV-2362, 2016 WL 2622372 (M.D. Pa. May 9, 2016) and FTC v. Advocate Health Network, No. 15 C 11473, 2016 WL 3387163 (N.D. Ill. June 20, 2016). In both cases, the courts rejected the FTC's assertion that the anticompetitive effects of the merger would be felt in narrow local geographic markets. The FTC has announced its plans to appeal both cases.

2. Managed Care Mergers

Add at page 1268 at the end of the first full paragraph:

The almost simultaneous announcements in 2015 of the proposed mergers of Aetna Inc. with Humana Inc. and of Anthem, Inc. with Cigna Corp. initiated a series of Congressional hearings, an investigation by the Antitrust Division of the U.S. Department of Justice, and proceedings before a large number of state insurance departments. The two mergers would combine four of the "Big 5" commercial insurance companies in the country. On July 21, 2016, the Justice Department along with a number of state attorneys general filed two suits asking the district court for the District of Columbia seeking to enjoin the mergers. U.S. Dep't Justice, Press Release (July 21, 2016) https://www.justice.gov/opa/pr/justice-department-and-state-attorneys-general-sue-block-anthem-s-acquisition-cigna-aetna-s. The government alleged the mergers would lessen competition in a variety of markets including the Medicare Advantage, individual, public exchange, large group, and national account markets. The Missouri Department of Insurance has issued a preliminary order that bars Aetna from offering certain plans if the merger goes forward, and the California Department of Insurance has urged the Department of Justice to block the Anthem/Cigna combination; however, both mergers have been approved by a majority of state insurance regulators with supervisory responsibility.

Apart from the complex antitrust issues raised by these mergers (which if they go to trial and appeal may stretch on for over six months), they also pose important policy questions. Should provider and payor mergers be tolerated on the theory that the "countervailing power" of the two sides balance out? Does the impetus to integrate fostered by the ACA justify such mergers? What might states do to mitigate the impact of provider or payor dominance? See Thomas L. Greaney, Dubious Health Care Merger Justifications—The Sumo Wrestler and "Government Made Me Do It" Defenses, Health Affairs Blog (Feb. 24, 2015); Erin C. Fuse Brown & Jaime S. King, The Double Edged Sword of Health Care Integration: Consolidation and Cost Control, ___ Ind. L. J.___ (2016).

3.   Physician Practice Mergers

Add at page 1269 at end of first full paragraph:

SAINT ALPHONSUS MEDICAL CENTER-NAMPA INC.; FEDERAL TRADE COMMISSION & STATE OF IDAHO V. ST. LUKE'S HEALTH SYSTEM

United States Court of Appeals, Ninth Circuit, 2015.
778 F.3d 775.

HURWITZ, CIRCUIT JUDGE:

This case arises out of the 2012 merger of two health care providers in Nampa, Idaho. The Federal Trade Commission and the State of Idaho sued, alleging that the merger violated § 7 of the Clayton Act, [ ], and state law; two local hospitals filed a similar complaint. Although the district court believed that the merger was intended to improve patient outcomes and might well do so, the judge nonetheless found that the merger violated § 7 and ordered divestiture.

As the district court recognized, the job before us is not to determine the optimal future shape of the country's health care system, but instead to determine whether this particular merger violates the Clayton Act. In light of the careful factual findings by the able district judge, we affirm the judgment below.

I.   Background

A.   *The Health Care Market in Nampa, Idaho*

Nampa, the second-largest city in Idaho, is some twenty miles west of Boise and has a population of approximately 85,000. Before the merger at issue, St. Luke's Health Systems, Ltd. ("St. Luke's"), an Idaho-based, not-for-profit health care system, operated an emergency clinic in the city. Saltzer Medical Group, P.A. ("Saltzer"), the largest independent multi-specialty physician group in Idaho, had thirty-four physicians practicing at its offices in Nampa. The only hospital in Nampa was operated by Saint Alphonsus Health System, Inc. ("Saint Alphonsus"), a part of the multistate Trinity Health system. Saint Alphonsus and Treasure Valley

Hospital Limited Partnership ("TVH") jointly operated an outpatient surgery center.

The largest adult primary care physician ("PCP") provider in the Nampa market was Saltzer, which had sixteen PCPs. St. Luke's had eight PCPs and Saint Alphonsus nine. Several other PCPs had solo or small practices.

B. *The Challenged Acquisition*

Saltzer had long had the goal of moving toward integrated patient care and risk-based reimbursement. After unsuccessfully attempting several informal affiliations, including one with St. Luke's, Saltzer sought a formal partnership with a large health care system.

[St. Luke's acquired Saltzer's assets and entered into a five-year professional service agreement ("PSA") with the Saltzer physicians in 2012. After St. Alphonsus and TVH filed a complaint seeking to enjoin the merger, the district court denied a motion for a preliminary injunction based on a commitment in the PSA providing a process for unwinding the transaction if it were declared illegal. Subsequently, after the FTC and the State of Idaho filed a complaint in the district court to enjoin the merger, the court consolidated the two cases and after a 19-day bench trial found the merger prohibited by the Clayton Act and the Idaho Competition Act because of its anticompetitive effects on the Nampa adult PCP market.]

The district court expressly noted the troubled state of the U.S. health care system, found that St. Luke's and Saltzer genuinely intended to move toward a better health care system, and expressed its belief that the merger would "improve patient outcomes" if left intact. Nonetheless, the court found that the "huge market share" of the post-merger entity "creates a substantial risk of anticompetitive price increases" in the Nampa adult PCP market. Rejecting an argument by St. Luke's that anticipated post-merger efficiencies excused the potential anticompetitive price effects, the district court ordered divestiture. This appeal followed.

* * *

B. *The Relevant Market*

[Defendants did not contest on appeal the district court's holding that the relevant product market was "adult PCP services which include physician services provided to commercially insured patients aged 18 and over by physicians practicing internal medicine, family practice, and general practice." The court of appeals upheld the district court's finding that the Adult PCP geographic market was local, noting testimony that Nampa residents "strongly prefer access to local PCPs" and that "commercial health plans need to include Nampa PCPs in their networks to offer a competitive product." Although one-third of Nampa residents travel to Boise for PCPs, it concluded that fact did not prove that a significant number of other residents would so travel in the event of a price increase because those who traveled generally went to PCPs near their Boise places of employment.]

* * *

[The court of appeals went on to summarize the district court's findings regarding pre- and post-merger market concentration. The court calculated post-merger HHI in the Nampa PCP market as 6,219 and the increase as 1,607, noting that these HHI numbers "are well above the thresholds for a presumptively anticompetitive merger (more than double and seven times their respective [DOJ/FTC Merger Guidelines] thresholds, respectively).")]

* * *

2. PCP Reimbursements

The district court also found that St. Luke's would likely use its post-merger power to negotiate higher reimbursement rates from insurers for PCP services. Recognizing that the § 7 inquiry is based on a prediction of future actions, *see Phila. Nat'l Bank,* 374 U.S. at 362, 83 S.Ct. 1715, this finding was not clearly erroneous.

Because St. Luke's and Saltzer had been each other's closest substitutes in Nampa, the district court found the acquisition limited the ability of insurers to negotiate with the merged entity. Pre-acquisition internal correspondence indicated that the merged companies would use this increased bargaining power to raise prices. An email between St. Luke's executives discussed "pressur[ing] payors for new directed agreements," and an exchange between Saltzer executives stated that "[i]f our negotiations w/ Luke's go to fruition," then "the clout of the entire network" could be used to negotiate favorable terms with insurers. The court also examined a previous acquisition by St. Luke's in Twin Falls, Idaho, and found that St. Luke's used its leverage in that instance to force insurers to "concede to their pricing proposal."

* * *

4. The Prima Facie Case

... [T]he district court's conclusion that a prima facie case was established is amply supported by the record. "Section 7 does not require proof that a merger or other acquisition has caused higher prices in the affected market. All that is necessary is that the merger create an appreciable danger of such consequences in the future." [ ]

The extremely high HHI on its own establishes the prima facie case. [ ] In addition, the court found that statements and past actions by the merging parties made it likely that St. Luke's would raise reimbursement rates in a highly concentrated market. [ ] And, the court's uncontested finding of high entry barriers "eliminates the possibility that the reduced competition caused by the merger will be ameliorated by new competition from outsiders and further strengthens the FTC's case."

* * *

D. *The Rebuttal Case*

Because the plaintiffs established a prima facie case, the burden shifted to St. Luke's to "cast doubt on the accuracy of the Government's evidence as predictive of future anticompetitive effects." [ ] The rebuttal evidence focused on the alleged procompetitive effects of the merger, particularly the contention that the merger would allow St. Luke's to move toward integrated care and risk-based reimbursement.

1. *The Post-Merger Efficiencies Defense*

The Supreme Court has never expressly approved an efficiencies defense to a § 7 claim. *See H.J. Heinz,* 246 F.3d at 720. Indeed, *Brown Shoe* cast doubt on the defense:

> Of course, some of the results of large integrated or chain operations are beneficial to consumers. Their expansion is not rendered unlawful by the mere fact that small independent stores may be adversely affected. It is competition, not competitors, which the Act protects. But we cannot fail to recognize Congress' desire to promote competition through the protection of viable, small, locally owned business. Congress appreciated that occasional higher costs and prices might result from the maintenance of fragmented industries and markets. It resolved these competing considerations in favor of decentralization. We must give effect to that decision.

370 U.S. at 344, 82 S.Ct. 1502. Similarly, in *FTC v. Procter & Gamble Co.,* the Court stated that "[p]ossible economies cannot be used as a defense to illegality. Congress was aware that some mergers which lessen competition may also result in economies but it struck the balance in favor of protecting competition." 386 U.S. 568, 580, 87 S.Ct. 1224, 18 L.Ed.2d 303 (1967).

Notwithstanding the Supreme Court's statements, four of our sister circuits (the Sixth, D.C., Eighth, and Eleventh) have suggested that proof of post-merger efficiencies could rebut a Clayton Act § 7 prima facie case. [ ] The FTC has also cautiously recognized the defense, noting that although competition ordinarily spurs firms to achieve efficiencies internally, "a primary benefit of mergers to the economy is their potential to generate significant efficiencies and thus enhance the merged firm's ability and incentive to compete, which may result in lower prices, improved quality, enhanced service, or new products." Merger Guidelines § 10 [ ]. However, none of the reported appellate decisions have actually held that a § 7 defendant has rebutted a prima facie case with an efficiencies defense; thus, even in those circuits that recognize it, the parameters of the defense remain imprecise.

* * *

We remain skeptical about the efficiencies defense in general and about its scope in particular. [The court cited several prominent Chicago School judges who expressed skepticism about courts' ability to weigh efficiencies in merger cases.] . . .

Nonetheless, we assume, as did the district court, that because § 7 of the Clayton Act only prohibits those mergers whose effect "may be substantially to lessen competition," 15 U.S.C. § 18, a defendant can rebut a prima facie case with evidence that the proposed merger will create a more efficient combined entity and thus increase competition. . . .

* * *

2.   *The St. Luke's Efficiencies Defense*

St. Luke's argues that the merger would benefit patients by creating a team of employed physicians with access to Epic, the electronic medical records system used by St. Luke's. The district court found that, even if true, these predicted efficiencies were insufficient to carry St. Luke's' burden of rebutting the prima facie case. We agree.

It is not enough to show that the merger would allow St. Luke's to better serve patients. The Clayton Act focuses on competition, and the claimed efficiencies therefore must show that the prediction of anticompetitive effects from the prima facie case is inaccurate. [ ] Although the district court believed that the merger would eventually "improve the delivery of health care" in the Nampa market, the judge did not find that the merger would increase competition or decrease prices. Quite to the contrary, the court, even while noting the likely beneficial effect of the merger on patient care, held that reimbursement rates for PCP services likely would increase. Nor did the court find that the merger would likely lead to integrated health care or a new reimbursement system; the judge merely noted the desire of St. Luke's to move in that direction.

The district court expressly did conclude, however, that the claimed efficiencies were not merger-specific. The court found "no empirical evidence to support the theory that St. Luke's needs a core group of employed primary care physicians beyond the number it had before the Acquisition to successfully make the transition to integrated care," and that "a committed team can be assembled without employing physicians." The court also found that the shared electronic record was not a merger-specific benefit because data analytics tools are available to independent physicians.

These factual findings were not clearly erroneous. Testimony highlighted examples of independent physicians who had adopted risk-based reimbursement, even though they were not employed by a major health system. The record also revealed that independent physicians had access to a number of analytic tools, including the St. Luke's Epic system.

But even if we assume that the claimed efficiencies were merger-specific, the defense would nonetheless fail. At most, the district court concluded that St. Luke's might provide better service to patients after the merger. That is a laudable goal, but the Clayton Act does not excuse mergers that lessen competition or create monopolies simply because the merged entity can improve its operations. [ ] The district court did not clearly err in concluding that whatever else St. Luke's proved, it did not demonstrate that efficiencies resulting from the merger would have a positive effect on competition.

IV. Remedy

* * *

. . . [T]he district court did not abuse its discretion in choosing divestiture over St. Luke's' proposed "conduct remedy"—the establishment of separate bargaining groups to negotiate with insurers. Divestiture is "simple, relatively easy to administer, and sure," [ ] while conduct remedies risk excessive government entanglement in the market, *see* U.S. Dep't of Justice, *Antitrust Division Policy Guide to Merger Remedies* § II n. 12 (2011) (noting that conduct remedies need to be "tailored as precisely as possible to the competitive harms associated with the merger to avoid unnecessary entanglements with the competitive process"). The district court, moreover, found persuasive the rejection of a similar proposal in *In re ProMedica Health System, Inc.* [ ] Even assuming that the district court might have been within its discretion in opting for a conduct remedy, we find no abuse of discretion in its declining to do so. *See ProMedica,* 749 F.3d at 572–73 (holding that the FTC did not abuse its discretion in choosing divestiture over a proposed conduct remedy).

V. Conclusion

For the reasons stated above, we AFFIRM the judgment of the district court.

NOTES AND QUESTIONS

1.   Is the Ninth Circuit's rejections of efficiencies at odds with the strong incentives for provider integration found in the Affordable Care Act and new Medicare reimbursement policies? Can those initiatives succeed in markets dominated by dominant hospitals or physician groups?

2.   Note that the district court and Ninth Circuit did not address claims made by a rival hospital that the acquisition of Saltzer also violated the

Clayton Act on a vertical theory: i.e., that by acquiring the lion's share of primary care physicians, St. Luke's would effectively foreclose competition in the hospital market as the rival would not receive referrals from employed physicians. Vertical challenges of this sort have been rare and impose high hurdles for plaintiffs. See Thomas L. Greaney & Douglas Ross, Navigating Through the Fog of Vertical Merger Law: A Guide to Counselling Hospital-Physician Consolidation Under the Clayton Act, 91 Wash. L. Rev. 199 (2016).

CHAPTER 15

REPRODUCTION AND BIRTH

■ ■ ■

III. CONTRACEPTION, ABORTION, AND STERILIZATION

A. CONTRACEPTION

Add at page 1302 after *Note: Coverage of Contraception Under the ACA*:

HOBBY LOBBY AND *ZUBIK*: AN UPDATE ON THE SUPREME COURT AND CONTRACEPTION UNDER THE AFFORDABLE CARE ACT

The ACA regulations required coverage of some forms of contraception that some employers and religious groups found to be forms of abortion, and thus unacceptable for religious reasons. See the *Note: The Blurry Distinction Between Contraception and Abortion* on page 1291. Churches themselves were exempt from this coverage. Regulations requiring this coverage were challenged by two groups of employers—non-profit religious organizations (other than churches themselves) and for-profit corporations that were run consistently with religious principles. The non-profit religious organizations, like religiously sponsored colleges and hospitals that had students or patients of many faiths, were allowed to opt out of providing contraceptive coverage for their employees by formally announcing that they had religious objections to offering this coverage. The announcement itself would trigger a process by which the health insurer itself, not the religious employer, would be required to provide the contraceptive coverage.

The for-profit corporations whose owners operated them in accord with religious principles were not entitled to any accommodation and given no "opt out" corridor. Some of the non-profits and for-profits argued that it would make them complicit in the sinful activity to provide contraceptive coverage, or even to formally opt out, if opting out would lead to the ultimate provision of the unacceptable coverage.

A case brought by an objecting for-profit corporation was the first to make it to the Supreme Court. In Burwell v. Hobby Lobby, Inc., 134 S.Ct. 2751 (2014), the Supreme Court determined that closely held private corporations could assert the religious liberty interests of their owners, and that the Affordable Care Act's mandate to provide contraception was a violation of the federal Religious Freedom Restoration Act (RFRA), as amended by the Religious Land Use and Institutionalized Persons Act (RLUIPA). The Court did not rest its holding on the First Amendment's free exercise clause because the ACA and the regulations issued under it were neutral laws of general applicability—they were not aimed at a religious practice, and they applied equally to everyone. See Employment Division v. Smith, 494 U.S. 872 (1990), holding that this was all that was required to meet the requirements of the free exercise clause. Congress had responded to the limited scope of the free exercise clause under *Smith* by passing RFRA (and, later, RLUIPA to address a problem in the original RFRA). RFRA required the courts to apply strict scrutiny to federal regulations like those in question; any substantial burden on the exercise of religion would be permitted only if there were a compelling government interest being served, and, even then, only if the interest could not be served in any less restrictive way. Effectively, through RFRA Congress re-established the strict scrutiny standard that had applied to Constitutional free exercise challenges before *Smith,* but only for free exercise actions against the federal government itself, not for actions against states.

Justice Alito, who wrote for the 5–4 majority finding that the contraceptive mandate violated RFRA, summarized his opinion this way:

> We must decide in these cases whether the Religious Freedom Restoration Act ... (RFRA) [] permits the United States Department of Health and Human Services (HHS) to demand that three closely held corporations provide health-insurance coverage for methods of contraception that violate the sincerely held religious beliefs of the companies' owners. We hold that the regulations that impose this obligation violate RFRA, which prohibits the Federal Government from taking any action that substantially burdens the exercise of religion unless that action constitutes the least restrictive means of serving a compelling government interest.

> In holding that the HHS mandate is unlawful, we reject HHS's argument that the owners of the companies forfeited all RFRA protection when they decided to organize their businesses as corporations rather than sole proprietorships or general partnerships. The plain terms of RFRA make it perfectly clear that Congress did not discriminate in this way against men and women who wish to run their businesses as for-profit corporations in the manner required by their religious beliefs.

> Since RFRA applies in these cases, we must decide whether the challenged HHS regulations substantially burden the exercise of religion, and we hold that they do. The owners of the businesses

have religious objections to abortion, and according to their religious beliefs the four contraceptive methods at issue are abortifacients. If the owners comply with the HHS mandate, they believe they will be facilitating abortions, and if they do not comply, they will pay a very heavy price—as much as $1.3 million per day, or about $475 million per year, in the case of one of the companies. If these consequences do not amount to a substantial burden, it is hard to see what would.

Under RFRA, a Government action that imposes a substantial burden on religious exercise must serve a compelling government interest, and we assume that the HHS regulations satisfy this requirement. But in order for the HHS mandate to be sustained, it must also constitute the least restrictive means of serving that interest, and the mandate plainly fails that test. There are other ways in which Congress or HHS could equally ensure that every woman has cost-free access to the particular contraceptives at issue here and, indeed, to all FDA-approved contraceptives.

In fact, HHS has already devised and implemented a system that seeks to respect the religious liberty of religious nonprofit corporations while ensuring that the employees of these entities have precisely the same access to all FDA-approved contraceptives as employees of companies whose owners have no religious objections to providing such coverage. [Ed. Note: This refers to the opt-out regulatory scheme, described above, that reached the Court two years later in *Zubik*, described below.] The employees of these religious nonprofit corporations still have access to insurance coverage without cost sharing for all FDA-approved contraceptives; and according to HHS, this system imposes no net economic burden on the insurance companies that are required to provide or secure the coverage.

Although HHS has made this system available to religious nonprofits that have religious objections to the contraceptive mandate, HHS has provided no reason why the same system cannot be made available when the owners of for-profit corporations have similar religious objections. We therefore conclude that this system constitutes an alternative that achieves all of the Government's aims while providing greater respect for religious liberty. And under RFRA, that conclusion means that enforcement of the HHS contraceptive mandate against the objecting parties in these cases is unlawful.

As this description of our reasoning shows, our holding is very specific. We do not hold, as the principal dissent alleges, that for-profit corporations and other commercial enterprises can "opt out of any law (saving only tax laws) they judge incompatible with their sincerely held religious beliefs." [ ] (opinion of Ginsburg, J.). Nor do we hold, as the dissent implies, that such corporations have free rein to take steps that impose "disadvantages . . . on others" or that require "the general public [to] pick up the tab." [ ] And we certainly do not hold or suggest that "RFRA demands accommodation of a for-profit corporation's religious beliefs no matter the impact that accommodation may have on . . . thousands of women employed by Hobby Lobby." [ ] The effect of the HHS-created accommodation on the women employed by Hobby Lobby and the other companies involved in these cases would be precisely zero. Under that accommodation, these women would still be entitled to all FDA-approved contraceptives without cost sharing.

Burwell v. Hobby Lobby, Inc., 134 S.Ct. 2751, 2759–60 (2014).

Independently, courts across the country were also considering the challenges to the opt-out process raised by religiously affiliated non-profits. They argued that the requirement that they either provide coverage for contraception or submit a formal written document asking to be relieved of the obligation violated RFRA, and different federal courts reached different conclusions on whether the opt-out requirement was a substantial burden, on whether the governmental interest was compelling, and on whether there was a less restrictive way of serving the same interest. After *Hobby Lobby*, many thought the issue was resolved because the Court seemed to depend so heavily on the existence of the non-profit opt-out provision in determining that there was a less burdensome alternative available to the government with regard to for-profits. The Supreme Court consolidated several non-profit challenges under the caption *Zubik v. Burwell* and scheduled argument for early 2016.

When Justice Scalia died shortly before the argument in 2016, many predicted that the Court would be equally divided on this issue. Following argument, the Court asked for supplemental briefing on whether there might be some way to reach a compromise by allowing the religious organizations to signal that they did not want their purchased insurance to include coverage of contraception, and for the insurance companies and the health plan administrators to then provide the contraception coverage independently, informing those covered that the contraception coverage was not requested by, administered by, or paid for by the religiously affiliated organization. When both the government and the plaintiffs filed responses to the request for supplemental briefs suggesting that such an arrangement would be possible, the Court remanded the several consolidated cases to the Courts of Appeals that had heard them earlier to find a practical way to satisfy the interests of both sides.

B. ABORTION

Add at page 1344 following *Notes and Questions*:

WHOLE WOMAN'S HEALTH V. HELLERSTEDT
Supreme Court of the United States, 2016.
136 S.Ct. 2292.

JUSTICE BREYER delivered the opinion of the Court.

In *Planned Parenthood of Southeastern Pa. v. Casey* [ ] a plurality of the Court concluded that there "exists" an "undue burden" on a woman's right to decide to have an abortion, and consequently a provision of law is constitutionally invalid, if the "*purpose or effect*" of the provision "*is to place a substantial obstacle* in the path of a woman seeking an abortion before the fetus attains viability." [ ] The plurality added that "[u]nnecessary health regulations that have the purpose or effect of presenting a substantial obstacle to a woman seeking an abortion impose an undue burden on the right." [ ]

We must here decide whether two provisions of Texas' House Bill 2 violate the Federal Constitution as interpreted in *Casey*. The first provision, which we shall call the "*admitting-privileges requirement*," says that

"[a] physician performing or inducing an abortion . . . must, on the date the abortion is performed or induced, have active admitting privileges at a hospital that . . . is located not further than 30 miles from the location at which the abortion is performed or induced." [ ]

This provision amended Texas law that had previously required an abortion facility to maintain a written protocol "for managing medical emergencies and the transfer of patients requiring further emergency care to a hospital." [ ]

The second provision, which we shall call the "*surgical-center requirement*," says that

"the minimum standards for an abortion facility must be equivalent to the minimum standards adopted under [the Texas Health and Safety Code section] for ambulatory surgical centers."
[ ]

We conclude that neither of these provisions confers medical benefits sufficient to justify the burdens upon access that each imposes. Each places a substantial obstacle in the path of women seeking a previability abortion, each constitutes an undue burden on abortion access, [ ], and each violates the Federal Constitution. [ ]

I

A

In July 2013, the Texas Legislature enacted House Bill 2 [which is the subject of this litigation. A part of the Act, the admitting-privileges provision, was challenged on its face in *Planned Parenthood of Greater Tex. Surgical Health Servs. v. Abbott*. Ultimately, the Fifth Circuit upheld that provision, and no review was sought in the Supreme Court.]

* * *

B

[One] week after the Fifth Circuit's decision, petitioners, a group of abortion providers (many of whom were plaintiffs in the previous lawsuit), filed the present lawsuit in Federal District Court. They sought an injunction preventing enforcement of the admitting-privileges provision as applied to physicians at two abortion facilities * * * . They also sought an injunction prohibiting enforcement of the surgical-center provision anywhere in Texas. They claimed that the admitting-privileges provision and the surgical-center provision violated the Constitution's Fourteenth Amendment, as interpreted in *Casey*.

The District Court subsequently received stipulations from the parties and depositions from the parties' experts. The court conducted a 4-day bench trial. It heard, among other testimony, the opinions from expert witnesses for both sides. On the basis of the stipulations, depositions, and testimony, that court reached the following conclusions:

1. Of Texas' population of more than 25 million people, "approximately 5.4 million" are "women" of "reproductive age," living within a geographical area of "nearly 280,000 square miles." [ ]

2. "In recent years, the number of abortions reported in Texas has stayed fairly consistent at approximately 15–16% of the reported pregnancy rate, for a total number of approximately 60,000–72,000 legal abortions performed annually." [ ]

3. Prior to the enactment of H.B. 2, there were more than 40 licensed abortion facilities in Texas, which "number dropped by almost half leading up to and in the wake of enforcement of the admitting-privileges requirement that went into effect in late-October 2013." [ ]

4. If the surgical-center provision were allowed to take effect, the number of abortion facilities, after September 1, 2014, would be reduced further, so that "only seven facilities and a potential eighth will exist in Texas." [ ]

* * *

7. The suggestion "that these seven or eight providers could meet the demand of the entire state stretches credulity." [ ]

8.   * * * After September 2014, should the surgical-center requirement go into effect, the number of women of reproductive age living significant distances from an abortion provider will increase [substantially]. [ ]

9.   The "two requirements erect a particularly high barrier for poor, rural, or disadvantaged women." [ ]

10.   "The great weight of evidence demonstrates that, before the act's passage, abortion in Texas was extremely safe with particularly low rates of serious complications and virtually no deaths occurring on account of the procedure." [ ]

11.   "Abortion, as regulated by the State before the enactment of House Bill 2, has been shown to be much safer, in terms of minor and serious complications, than many common medical procedures not subject to such intense regulation and scrutiny." [ ].

12.   "Additionally, risks are not appreciably lowered for patients who undergo abortions at ambulatory surgical centers as compared to nonsurgical-center facilities." [ ].

13.   "[W]omen will not obtain better care or experience more frequent positive outcomes at an ambulatory surgical center as compared to a previously licensed facility." [ ]

* * *

On the basis of these and other related findings, the District Court determined that the surgical-center requirement "imposes an undue burden on the right of women throughout Texas to seek a previability abortion," and that the "admitting-privileges requirement, . . . in conjunction with the ambulatory-surgical-center requirement, imposes an undue burden on the right of women * * * to seek a previability abortion." [ ] The District Court concluded that the "two provisions" would cause "the closing of almost all abortion clinics in Texas that were operating legally in the fall of 2013," and thereby create a constitutionally "impermissible obstacle as applied to all women seeking a previability abortion" by "restricting access to previously available legal facilities." [ ] [T]he court enjoined the enforcement of the two provisions.

C

* * *

[T]he Court of Appeals reversed the District Court on the merits. With minor exceptions, it found both provisions constitutional and allowed them to take effect. [ ]

* * *

II

[In this part of the Opinion, the Court explains why the plaintiffs' claims are not barred by the doctrine of *res judicata*, also known as claims preclusion.]

* * *

III

Undue Burden—Legal Standard

We begin with the standard, as described in *Casey.* We recognize that the "State has a legitimate interest in seeing to it that abortion, like any other medical procedure, is performed under circumstances that insure maximum safety for the patient." *Roe v. Wade,* [ ]. But, we added, "a statute which, while furthering [a] valid state interest, has the effect of placing a substantial obstacle in the path of a woman's choice cannot be considered a permissible means of serving its legitimate ends." *Casey,* [ ]. Moreover, "[u]nnecessary health regulations that have the purpose or effect of presenting a substantial obstacle to a woman seeking an abortion impose an undue burden on the right." [ ]

The Court of Appeals wrote that a state law is "constitutional if: (1) it does not have the purpose or effect of placing a substantial obstacle in the path of a woman seeking an abortion of a nonviable fetus; and (2) it is reasonably related to (or designed to further) a legitimate state interest." [ ] The Court of Appeals went on to hold that "the district court erred by substituting its own judgment for that of the legislature" when it conducted its "undue burden inquiry," in part because "medical uncertainty underlying a statute is for resolution by legislatures, not the courts." [ ]

The Court of Appeals' articulation of the relevant standard is incorrect. The first part of the Court of Appeals' test may be read to imply that a district court should not consider the existence or nonexistence of medical benefits when considering whether a regulation of abortion constitutes an undue burden. The rule announced in *Casey,* however, requires that courts consider the burdens a law imposes on abortion access together with the benefits those laws confer. [ ] And the second part of the test is wrong to equate the judicial review applicable to the regulation of a constitutionally protected personal liberty with the less strict review applicable where, for example, economic legislation is at issue. [ ] The Court of Appeals' approach simply does not match the standard that this Court laid out in *Casey,* which asks courts to consider whether any burden imposed on abortion access is "undue."

The statement that legislatures, and not courts, must resolve questions of medical uncertainty is also inconsistent with this Court's case law. Instead, the Court, when determining the constitutionality of laws regulating abortion procedures, has placed considerable weight upon evidence and argument presented in judicial proceedings. In *Casey,* for example, we relied heavily on the District Court's factual findings and the research-based submissions of *amici* in declaring a portion of the law at issue unconstitutional. [ ] (discussing evidence related to the prevalence of spousal abuse in determining that a spousal notification provision erected an undue burden to abortion access). And, in *Gonzales* the Court, while pointing out that we must review legislative "factfinding under a deferential standard," added that we must not "place dispositive weight" on those "findings." [ ] *Gonzales* went on to point out that the "*Court retains an independent constitutional duty to review factual findings where constitutional rights are at stake.*" [ ] (emphasis added). Although there we upheld a statute regulating abortion, we did not do so solely on the basis of legislative findings explicitly set forth in the statute, noting that "evidence presented in the District Courts contradicts" some of the legislative findings. [ ]. In these circumstances, we said, "[u]ncritical deference to Congress' factual findings . . . is inappropriate." [ ]

Unlike in *Gonzales,* the relevant statute here does not set forth any legislative findings. Rather, one is left to infer that the legislature sought to further a constitutionally acceptable objective (namely, protecting women's health). [ ] For a district court to give significant weight to evidence in the judicial record in these circumstances is consistent with this Court's case law. As we shall describe, the District Court did so here. It did not simply substitute its own judgment for that of the legislature. It considered the evidence in the record—including expert evidence, presented in stipulations, depositions, and testimony. It then weighed the asserted benefits against the burdens. We hold that, in so doing, the District Court applied the correct legal standard.

IV

Undue Burden—Admitting-Privileges Requirement

Turning to the lower courts' evaluation of the evidence, we first consider the admitting-privileges requirement. Before the enactment of H.B. 2, doctors who provided abortions were required to "have admitting privileges *or* have a working arrangement with a physician(s) who has admitting privileges at a local hospital in order to ensure the necessary back up for medical complications." [ ] The new law changed this requirement by requiring that a "physician performing or inducing an abortion . . . must, on the date the abortion is performed or induced, have active admitting privileges at a hospital that . . . is located not further than 30 miles from the location at which the abortion is performed or induced." [ ] The District Court held that the legislative change imposed an "undue burden" on a woman's right to have an abortion. We conclude that there is adequate legal and factual support for the District Court's conclusion.

The purpose of the admitting-privileges requirement is to help ensure that women have easy access to a hospital should complications arise during an abortion procedure. [ ] But the District Court found that it brought about no such health-related benefit. The court found that "[t]he great weight of evidence demonstrates that, before the act's passage, abortion in Texas was extremely safe with particularly low rates of serious complications and virtually no deaths occurring on account of the procedure." [ ]. Thus, there was no significant health-related problem that the new law helped to cure.

[The Court then summarized the evidence that drew the trial court to that conclusion.]

* * *

At the same time, the record evidence indicates that the admitting-privileges requirement places a "substantial obstacle in the path of a woman's choice." [ ] [The Court pointed out that the evidence showed that many clinics closed when the admitting-privileges requirement went into effect.]

* * *

[There are many] common prerequisites to obtaining admitting privileges that have nothing to do with ability to perform medical procedures. See Brief for Medical Staff Professionals as *Amici Curiae* [ ] (listing, for example, requirements that an applicant has treated a high number of patients in the hospital setting in the past year, clinical data requirements, residency requirements, and other discretionary factors); see also Brief for American College of Obstetricians and Gynecologists [ ] ("[S]ome academic hospitals will only allow medical staff membership for clinicians who also . . . accept faculty appointments"). Again, returning to the District Court record, we note that Dr. Lynn of the McAllen clinic, a veteran obstetrics and gynecology doctor who estimates that he has delivered over 15,000 babies in his 38 years in practice was unable to get admitting privileges at any of the seven hospitals within 30 miles of his clinic. [ ]. He was refused admitting privileges at a nearby hospital for reasons, as the hospital wrote, "not based on clinical competence considerations." [ ] The admitting-privileges requirement does not serve any relevant credentialing function.

In our view, the record contains sufficient evidence that the admitting-privileges requirement led to the closure of half of Texas' clinics, or thereabouts. Those closures meant fewer doctors, longer waiting times, and increased crowding. Record evidence also supports the finding that after the admitting-privileges provision went into effect, the "number of women of reproductive age living in a county . . . more than 150 miles from a provider increased from approximately 86,000 to 400,000 . . . and the number of women living in a county more than 200 miles from a provider from approximately 10,000 to 290,000." [ ]. We recognize that increased driving distances do not always constitute an "undue burden." [ ] But here, those increases are but one additional burden, which, when taken together with others that the closings brought about, and when viewed in light of the virtual absence of any health benefit, lead us to conclude that the record adequately supports the District Court's "undue burden" conclusion. [ ]

* * *

[T]he dissent suggests that one benefit of H.B. 2's requirements would be that they might "force unsafe facilities to shut down." [ ] To support that assertion, the dissent points to the Kermit Gosnell scandal. Gosnell, a physician in Pennsylvania, was convicted of first-degree murder and manslaughter [as a result of the operation of an abortion clinic]. * * * Gosnell's behavior was terribly wrong. But there is no reason to believe that an extra layer of regulation would have affected that behavior. Determined wrongdoers, already ignoring existing statutes and safety measures, are unlikely to be convinced to adopt safe practices by a new overlay of regulations. * * * The record contains nothing to suggest that H.B. 2 would be more effective than pre-existing Texas law at deterring wrongdoers like Gosnell from criminal behavior.

V

Undue Burden—Surgical-Center Requirement

The second challenged provision of Texas' new law sets forth the surgical-center requirement. Prior to enactment of the new requirement, Texas law required abortion facilities to meet a host of health and safety requirements [which are listed in the opinion by the court]. * * *

H.B. 2 added the requirement that an "abortion facility" meet the "minimum standards . . . for ambulatory surgical centers" under Texas law. [ ] The surgical-center regulations include, among other things, detailed specifications relating to the size of the nursing staff, building dimensions, and other building requirements. [The Court went on to list the many requirements imposed on surgical-centers.]

There is considerable evidence in the record supporting the District Court's findings indicating that the statutory provision requiring all abortion facilities to meet all surgical-center standards does not benefit patients and is not necessary. The District Court found that "risks are not appreciably lowered for patients who undergo abortions at ambulatory surgical centers as compared to nonsurgical-center facilities." [ ] The court added that women "will not obtain better care or experience more frequent positive outcomes at an ambulatory surgical center as compared to a previously licensed facility." [ ] And these findings are well supported.

The record makes clear that the surgical-center requirement provides no benefit when complications arise in the context of an abortion produced through medication. That is because, in such a case, complications would almost always arise only after the patient has left the facility. [ ] The record also contains evidence indicating that abortions taking place in an abortion facility are safe—indeed, safer than numerous procedures that take place outside hospitals and to which Texas does not apply its surgical-center requirements. * * * Nationwide, childbirth is 14 times more likely than abortion to result in death, [ ] but Texas law allows a midwife to oversee childbirth in the patient's own home. Colonoscopy, a procedure that typically takes place outside a hospital (or surgical center) setting, has a mortality rate 10 times higher than an abortion. [T]he mortality rate for liposuction, another outpatient procedure, is 28 times higher than the mortality rate for abortion. Medical treatment after an incomplete miscarriage often involves a procedure identical to that involved in a nonmedical abortion, but it often takes place outside a hospital or surgical center. And Texas partly or wholly grandfathers (or waives in whole or in part the surgical-center requirement for) about two-thirds of the facilities to which the surgical-center standards apply. But it neither grandfathers nor provides waivers for any of the facilities that perform abortions. [ ] These facts indicate that the surgical-center provision imposes "a requirement that simply is not based on differences" between abortion and other surgical procedures "that are reasonably related to" preserving women's health, the asserted "purpos[e] of the Act in which it is found." [ ]

* * *

At the same time, the record provides adequate evidentiary support for the District Court's conclusion that the surgical-center requirement places a substantial obstacle in the path of women seeking an abortion. The parties stipulated that the requirement would further reduce the number of abortion facilities available to seven or eight facilities * * * . In the District Court's view, the proposition that these "seven or eight providers could meet the demand of the entire State stretches credulity." [ ] We take this statement as a finding that these few facilities could not "meet" that "demand."

The Court of Appeals held that this finding was "clearly erroneous." * * * [W]e hold that the record provides adequate support for the District Court's finding.

* * *

More fundamentally, in the face of no threat to women's health, Texas seeks to force women to travel long distances to get abortions in crammed-to-capacity superfacilities. Patients seeking these services are less likely to get the kind of individualized attention, serious conversation, and emotional support that doctors at less taxed facilities may have offered.

Healthcare facilities and medical professionals are not fungible commodities. Surgical centers attempting to accommodate sudden, vastly increased demand, [ ] may find that quality of care declines. Another commonsense inference that the District Court made is that these effects would be harmful to, not supportive of, women's health. [ ].

* * *

We agree with the District Court that the surgical-center requirement, like the admitting-privileges requirement, provides few, if any, health benefits for women, poses a substantial obstacle to women seeking abortions, and constitutes an "undue burden" on their constitutional right to do so.

VI

[In this section the Court explains why the severability clause is of no assistance to Texas in this case.]

JUSTICE GINSBURG, concurring.

The Texas law called H.B. 2 inevitably will reduce the number of clinics and doctors allowed to provide abortion services. Texas argues that H.B. 2's restrictions are constitutional because they protect the health of women who experience complications from abortions. In truth, "complications from an abortion are both rare and rarely dangerous." [ ] Many medical procedures, including childbirth, are far more dangerous to patients, yet are not subject to ambulatory-surgical-center or hospital admitting-privileges requirements. [ ] Given those realities, it is beyond rational belief that H.B. 2 could genuinely protect the health of women, and certain that the law "would simply make it more difficult for them to obtain abortions." [ ] When a State severely limits access to safe and legal procedures, women in desperate circumstances may resort to unlicensed rogue practitioners, *faute de mieux,* at great risk to their health and safety. [ ] So long as this Court adheres to *Roe v. Wade* [ ], and *Planned Parenthood of Southeastern Pa. v. Casey,* [ ] Targeted Regulation of Abortion Providers laws like H.B. 2 that "do little or nothing for health, but rather strew impediments to abortion," [ ] cannot survive judicial inspection.

JUSTICE THOMAS, dissenting.

Today the Court strikes down two state statutory provisions in all of their applications, at the behest of abortion clinics and doctors. That decision exemplifies the Court's troubling tendency "to bend the rules when any effort to limit abortion, or even to speak in opposition to abortion, is at issue." [ ] As JUSTICE ALITO observes, [ ] today's decision creates an abortion exception to ordinary rules of *res judicata*, ignores compelling evidence that Texas' law imposes no unconstitutional burden, and disregards basic principles of the severability doctrine. I write separately to emphasize how today's decision perpetuates the Court's habit of applying different rules to different constitutional rights—especially the putative right to abortion.

To begin, the very existence of this suit is a jurisprudential oddity. Ordinarily, plaintiffs cannot file suits to vindicate the constitutional rights of others. But the Court employs a different approach to rights that it favors. So in this case and many others, the Court has erroneously allowed doctors and clinics to vicariously vindicate the putative constitutional right of women seeking abortions.

This case also underscores the Court's increasingly common practice of invoking a given level of scrutiny—here, the abortion-specific undue burden standard—while applying a different standard of review entirely. Whatever scrutiny the majority applies to Texas' law, it bears little resemblance to the undue-burden test the Court articulated in *Planned Parenthood of Southeastern Pa. v. Casey,* [ ] and its successors. Instead, the majority eviscerates important features of that test to return to a regime like the one that *Casey* repudiated.

Ultimately, this case shows why the Court never should have bent the rules for favored rights in the first place. Our law is now so riddled with special exceptions for special rights that our decisions deliver neither predictability nor the promise of a judiciary bound by the rule of law.

I

This suit is possible only because the Court has allowed abortion clinics and physicians to invoke a putative constitutional right that does not belong to them—a woman's right to abortion. [Justice Thomas then explains why the medical plaintiffs in this case should not have standing to raise these claims, which really belong to women who seek abortions].

* * *

There should be no surer sign that our jurisprudence has gone off the rails than this: After creating a constitutional right to abortion because it "involve[s] the most intimate and personal choices a person may make in a lifetime, choices central to personal dignity and autonomy," [ ] the Court has created special rules that cede its enforcement to others.

II

Today's opinion also reimagines the undue-burden standard used to assess the constitutionality of abortion restrictions. Nearly 25 years ago, in *Planned Parenthood of Southeastern Pa. v. Casey,* [ ], a plurality of this Court invented the "undue burden" standard as a special test for gauging the permissibility of abortion restrictions. *Casey* held that a law is unconstitutional if it imposes an "undue burden" on a woman's ability to choose to have an abortion, meaning that it "has the purpose or effect of placing a substantial obstacle in the path of a woman seeking an abortion of a nonviable fetus." [ ] *Casey* thus instructed courts to look to whether a law substantially impedes women's access to abortion, and whether it is reasonably related to legitimate state interests. As the Court explained, "[w]here it has a rational basis to act, and it does not impose an undue burden, the State may use its regulatory power" to regulate aspects of abortion procedures, "all in furtherance of its legitimate interests in regulating the medical profession in order to promote respect for life, including life of the unborn." [ ]

I remain fundamentally opposed to the Court's abortion jurisprudence. [ ] Even taking *Casey* as the baseline, however, the majority radically rewrites the undue-burden test in three ways. First, today's decision requires courts to "consider the burdens a law imposes on abortion access together with the benefits those laws confer." [ ] Second, today's opinion tells the courts that, when the law's justifications are medically uncertain, they need not defer to the legislature, and must instead assess medical justifications for abortion restrictions by scrutinizing the record themselves. [ ] Finally, even if a law imposes no "substantial obstacle" to women's access to abortions, the law now must have more than a "reasonabl[e] relat[ion] to . . . a legitimate state interest." [ ] (internal quotation marks omitted). These precepts are nowhere to be found in *Casey* or its successors, and transform the undue-burden test to something much more akin to strict scrutiny.

First, the majority's free-form balancing test is contrary to *Casey*. * * * Contrary to the majority's statements [ ] *Casey* did not balance the benefits and burdens of Pennsylvania's spousal and parental notification provisions, either. Pennsylvania's spousal notification requirement, the plurality said, imposed an undue burden because findings established that the requirement would "likely . . . prevent a significant number of women from obtaining an abortion"—not because these burdens outweighed its benefits. [ ]. And *Casey* summarily upheld parental notification provisions because even pre-*Casey* decisions had done so. [ ]

* * *

Second, by rejecting the notion that "legislatures, and not courts, must resolve questions of medical uncertainty," [ ] the majority discards another core element of the *Casey* framework. Before today, this Court had "given state and federal legislatures wide discretion to pass legislation in areas where there is medical and scientific uncertainty." * * *

Today, however, the majority refuses to leave disputed medical science to the legislature because past cases "placed considerable weight upon the evidence and argument presented in judicial proceedings." * * *

Finally, the majority overrules another central aspect of *Casey* by requiring laws to have more than a rational basis even if they do not substantially impede access to abortion. [ ] "Where [the State] *has a rational basis to act* and it does not impose an undue burden," this Court previously held, "the State may use its regulatory power" to impose regulations "in furtherance of its legitimate interests in regulating the medical profession in order to promote respect for life, including life of the unborn." [ ] No longer. Though the majority declines to say how substantial a State's interest must be, [ ] one thing is clear: The State's burden has been ratcheted to a level that has not applied for a quarter century.

Today's opinion does resemble *Casey* in one respect: After disregarding significant aspects of the Court's prior jurisprudence, the majority applies the undue-burden standard in a way that will surely mystify lower courts for years to come. As in *Casey,* today's opinion "simply . . . highlight[s] certain facts in the record that apparently strike the . . . Justices as particularly significant in establishing (or refuting) the existence of an undue burden." [ ] As in *Casey,* "the opinion then simply announces that the provision either does or does not impose a 'substantial obstacle' or an 'undue burden.' " [ ] And still "[w]e do not know whether the same conclusions could have been reached on a different record, or in what respects the record would have had to differ before an opposite conclusion would have been appropriate. [ ] All we know is that an undue burden now has little to do with whether the law, in a "real sense, deprive[s] women of the ultimate decision," [ ] and more to do with the loss of "individualized attention, serious conversation, and emotional support," [ ].

The majority's undue-burden test looks far less like our post-*Casey* precedents and far more like the strict-scrutiny standard that *Casey* rejected, under which only the most compelling rationales justified restrictions on abortion. [ ] One searches the majority opinion in vain for any acknowledgment of the "premise central" to *Casey*'s rejection of strict scrutiny: "that the government has a legitimate and substantial interest in preserving and promoting fetal life" from conception, not just in regulating medical procedures. * * * Moreover, by second-guessing medical evidence and making its own assessments of "quality of care" issues, [ ] the majority reappoints this Court as "the country's *ex officio* medical board with powers to disapprove medical and operative practices and standards throughout the United States." [ ] And the majority seriously burdens States, which must guess at how much more compelling their interests must be to pass muster and what "commonsense inferences" of an undue burden this Court will identify next.

III

The majority's furtive reconfiguration of the standard of scrutiny applicable to abortion restrictions also points to a deeper problem. The undue-burden standard is just one variant of the Court's tiers-of-scrutiny approach to constitutional adjudication. And the label the Court affixes to its level of scrutiny in assessing whether the government can restrict a given right—be it "rational basis," intermediate, strict, or something else—is increasingly a meaningless formalism. As the Court applies whatever standard it likes to any given case, nothing but empty words separates our constitutional decisions from judicial fiat.

* * *

The Court should abandon the pretense that anything other than policy preferences underlies its balancing of constitutional rights and interests in any given case.

IV

It is tempting to identify the Court's invention of a constitutional right to abortion in *Roe v. Wade* [ ] as the tipping point that transformed third-party standing doctrine and the tiers of scrutiny into an unworkable morass of special exceptions and arbitrary applications. But those roots run deeper, to the very notion that some constitutional rights demand preferential treatment.

* * *

[Over the past 80 years, the] Court has simultaneously transformed judicially created rights like the right to abortion into preferred constitutional rights, while disfavoring many of the rights actually enumerated in the Constitution. But our Constitution renounces the notion that some constitutional rights are more equal than others. A plaintiff either possesses the constitutional right he is asserting, or not—and if not, the judiciary has no business creating ad hoc exceptions so that others can assert rights that seem especially important to vindicate. A law either infringes a constitutional right, or not; there is no room for the judiciary to invent tolerable degrees of encroachment. Unless the Court abides by one set of rules to adjudicate constitutional rights, it will continue reducing constitutional law to policy-driven value judgments until the last shreds of its legitimacy disappear.

* * *

I respectfully dissent.

JUSTICE ALITO, with whom THE CHIEF JUSTICE and JUSTICE THOMAS join, dissenting.

The constitutionality of laws regulating abortion is one of the most controversial issues in American law, but this case does not require us to delve into that contentious dispute. Instead, the dispositive issue here concerns a workaday question that can arise in any case no matter the subject, namely, whether the present case is barred by res judicata. As a court of law, we have an obligation to apply such rules in a neutral fashion in all cases, regardless of the subject of the suit. If anything, when a case involves a controversial issue, we should be especially careful to be scrupulously neutral in applying such rules.

The Court has not done so here. On the contrary, determined to strike down two provisions of a new Texas abortion statute in all of their applications, the Court simply disregards basic rules that apply in all other cases.

Here is the worst example. Shortly after Texas enacted House Bill 2 in 2013, the petitioners in this case brought suit, claiming, among other things, that a provision of the new law requiring a physician performing an abortion to have admitting privileges at a nearby hospital is "facially" unconstitutional and thus totally unenforeeable. Petitioners had a fair opportunity to make their case, but they lost on the merits in the United States Court of Appeals for the Fifth Circuit, and they chose not to petition this Court for review. The judgment against them became final. *Planned Parenthood of Greater Tex. Surgical Health Servs. v. Abbott,* 951 F.Supp.2d 891 (W.D.Tex.2013), aff'd in part and rev'd in part, 748 F.3d 583 (C.A.5 2014) (*Abbott*).

Under the rules that apply in regular cases, petitioners could not relitigate the exact same claim in a second suit. As we have said, "a losing litigant deserves no rematch after a defeat fairly suffered, in adversarial proceedings, on an issue identical in substance to the one he subsequently seeks to raise." [ ]

In this abortion case, however, that rule is disregarded. The Court awards a victory to petitioners on the very claim that they unsuccessfully pressed in the earlier case. The Court does this even though petitioners, undoubtedly realizing that a rematch would not be allowed, did not presume to include such a claim in their complaint. The Court favors petitioners with a victory that they did not have the audacity to seek.

Here is one more example: the Court's treatment of H.B. 2's "severability clause." When part of a statute is held to be unconstitutional, the question arises whether other parts of the statute must also go. If a statute says that provisions found to be unconstitutional can be severed from the rest of the statute, the valid provisions are allowed to stand. H.B. 2 contains what must surely be the most emphatic severability clause ever written. This clause says that every single word of the statute and every possible application of its provisions is severable. But despite this language, the Court holds that no part of the challenged provisions and no application of any part of them can be saved. Provisions that are indisputably constitutional—for example, provisions that require facilities performing abortions to follow basic fire safety measures—are stricken from the books. There is no possible justification for this collateral damage.

The Court's patent refusal to apply well-established law in a neutral way is indefensible and will undermine public confidence in the Court as a fair and neutral arbiter.

[In Parts I and II of his opinion, Justice Alito explains why the plaintiffs' challenges to the admitting-privileges requirements (Part I) and the surgical-center requirements (Part II) are barred by the doctrine of claim preclusion.]

III

Even if res judicata did not bar either facial claim, a sweeping, statewide injunction against the enforcement of the admitting privileges and ASC [i.e., surgical-center] requirements would still be unjustified. Petitioners in this case are abortion clinics and physicians who perform abortions. If they were simply asserting a constitutional right to conduct a business or to practice a profession without unnecessary state regulation, they would have little chance of success. [ ] Under our abortion cases, however, they are permitted to rely on the right of the abortion patients they serve. [ ]

Thus, what matters for present purposes is not the effect of the H.B. 2 provisions on petitioners but the effect on their patients. Under our cases, petitioners must show that the admitting privileges and ASC requirements impose an "undue burden" on women seeking abortions. *Gonzales v. Carhart,* [ ]. And in order to obtain the sweeping relief they seek—facial invalidation of those provisions—they must show, at a minimum, that these provisions have an unconstitutional impact on at least a "large fraction" of Texas women of reproductive age. [ ] Such a situation could result if the clinics able to comply with the new requirements either lacked the requisite overall capacity or were located too far away to serve a "large fraction" of the women in question.

Petitioners did not make that showing. Instead of offering direct evidence, they relied on two crude inferences. First, they pointed to the number of abortion clinics that closed after the enactment of H.B. 2, and asked that it be inferred that all these closures resulted from the two challenged provisions. [ ] They made little effort to show why particular clinics closed. Second, they pointed to the number of abortions performed annually at ASCs before H.B. 2 took effect and, because this figure is well below the total number of abortions performed each year in the State, they asked that it be inferred that ASC-compliant clinics could not meet the demands of women in the State. [ ] Petitioners failed to provide any evidence of the actual capacity of the facilities that would be available to perform abortions in compliance with the new law—even though they provided this type of evidence in their first case to the District Court at trial * * * .

IV

Even if the Court were right to hold that res judicata does not bar this suit and that H.B. 2 imposes an undue burden on abortion access—it is, in fact, wrong on both counts—it is still wrong to conclude that the admitting privileges and surgical center provisions must be enjoined in their entirety. H.B. 2 has an extraordinarily broad severability clause that must be considered before enjoining any portion or application of the law. Both challenged provisions should survive in substantial part if the Court faithfully applies that clause. Regrettably, it enjoins both in full, heedless of the (controlling) intent of the state legislature. [ ]

A

Applying H.B. 2's severability clause to the admitting privileges requirement is easy. Simply put, the requirement must be upheld in every city in which its application does not pose an undue burden. It surely does not pose that burden anywhere in the eastern half of the State, where most Texans live and where virtually no woman of reproductive age lives more than 150 miles from an open clinic. * * * And petitioners would need to show that the requirement caused specific West Texas clinics to close * * * .

B

Applying severability to the surgical center requirement calls for the identification of the particular provisions of the ASC regulations that result in the imposition of an undue burden. These regulations are lengthy and detailed, and while compliance with some might be expensive, compliance with many others would not. And many serve important health and safety purposes. Thus, the surgical center requirements cannot be judged as a package. But the District Court nevertheless held that all the surgical center requirements are unconstitutional in all cases, and the Court sustains this holding on grounds that are hard to take seriously.

* * *

By forgoing severability, the Court strikes down numerous provisions that could not plausibly impose an undue burden. For example, surgical center patients must "be treated with respect, consideration, and dignity." [ ] That's now enjoined. [Justice Alito gives several other examples of particular requirements, like fire and safety requirements, that are unlikely to be "undue burdens."]

* * * The Court's wholesale refusal to engage in the required severability analysis here revives the "antagonistic 'canon of construction under which in cases involving abortion, a permissible reading of a statute is to be avoided at all costs.'" [ ]

* * *

V

When we decide cases on particularly controversial issues, we should take special care to apply settled procedural rules in a neutral manner. The Court has not done that here.

I therefore respectfully dissent.

NOTES AND QUESTIONS

1.   Does *Whole Woman's Health* help you understand what constitutes a substantial obstacle in the pathway of a woman seeking an abortion, and thus is an undue burden on the exercise of a Constitutional right? How does it change the way that courts should analyze state statutes that have the purpose or effect of limiting access to abortion? Justice Breyer suggests that the test requires a balancing of the burdens imposed on the woman seeking the abortion with the benefits of the state law (in this case, the health benefits of the law). Is that balancing an appropriate task for the judiciary, or is it a role normally reserved for legislative bodies? Here, the Court found that there were no health benefits that came out of the state law, and that the law did limit some women's access to abortion, so the balancing was easy. What if there were some credible evidence that law provided some small health benefit? The dissents argue that there is no real standard to apply in doing the balancing, and that each Justice's personal policy views on the propriety of abortion necessarily (but inappropriately) must be dispositive. Are they right? Is there any alternative to balancing?

2.   Was the Texas legislature's fatal flaw their failure to make formal findings regarding the health benefits of H.B. 2 and include them in the text of the statute? If the legislature had done so, would the result have been different? Should it be? Even if those views were nothing more than a subterfuge to justify limitations on abortion? Could Texas now repass H.B. 2, but with a new preamble and specific factual findings about the health benefits it would confer on women in Texas? If you were advising a legislative body considering a new statute formally designed—honestly or dishonestly—to make abortions safer, what advice would you give them about drafting the statute?

3.   Although many legislative restrictions on abortion are justified on the argument that they will improve the health of women who seek abortions, not all are justified that way. As the dissenting Justices point out, there are other reasons—including the protection of the life of the fetus from conception to birth—that can justify restrictions on abortion access. How should *Whole Woman's Health* be applied to regulations that are not justified by their consequences on women's health? Does it help us determine the Constitutionality of state restrictions on health plans and insurance policies that discourage them from including abortion coverage? How about regulation of the informed consent process, including state laws that require women to undergo ultrasounds, and view them, before consenting to abortions? How

would you now analyze the Constitutional status of state laws that prohibit abortions for particular reasons—because of the gender or disability of the fetus, for example? Could laws that outlaw all abortions after 20 weeks of gestation survive Constitutional scrutiny? Could laws that require pain relief treatment for all fetuses over 18 weeks gestation that are aborted survive Constitutional scrutiny if the legislature makes findings that such fetuses can feel pain? Review the state legislation that is described on pages 1348–1349 of the casebook, and apply the *Whole Woman's Health* test to each of those proposals. Does it help you resolve those cases?

4.   The deep and abiding division on the Supreme Court with respect to abortion reflects the division across the country. Advocates on each side of the issue have shown those on the other side little respect, and, often, little civility. The mistrust between those on different sides of the issue is apparent in *Whole Woman's Health*. Justices Thomas and Alito argue that the Court treats abortion differently than it treats other substantive issues because the Court majority wants to vindicate its policy preference for the availability of abortions, not for any reason based on the Constitution. Essentially, the dissents argue that the majority is not only substantively wrong, but also prejudiced and dishonest with regard to their reasoning in abortion cases. Justice Ginsburg, on the other hand, refers to "Targeted Regulation of Abortion Providers" (caps in original) laws, the "TRAP laws" that pro-choice advocates believe are dishonestly supported by those who do not really care about the health of women at all, but who use arguments about their health as an excuse to limit access to abortion for religious, moral or other reasons. Why does each side believe that their opponents are arguing in bad faith? Has the political capital of the Supreme Court been squandered by continuing to hear abortion cases, in which the Justices accuse one another of intellectual dishonesty? Would it be squandered by a determination that it should cease recognizing such a right, after 45 years of doing so, because of the political division that surrounds it? Is there any way in which the Supreme Court could ameliorate the divisiveness of the abortion issue rather than exacerbate it?

5.   The foundation of the dissenting opinions in this case is that the majority ignored standard law on procedural issues—standing and claims preclusion—to get to a substantive issue that they wanted to address. Should abortion providers like Planned Parenthood have standing to raise the Constitutional rights of individual women on behalf of their patients? The alternative would be to require pregnant women to raise these claims under highly time-sensitive circumstances, and it is hard to imagine how an appropriate remedy could be fashioned in any particular case if clinics had already been forced to close. On the other hand, the dissents suggest that the Constitutional rights of the women involved have been subordinated to the corporate interests of the clinics and providers themselves by allowing the lawsuits to be controlled by those providers. What is the purpose of the standing requirement? How can that purpose be best served in cases testing state legislative limits on abortion?

6.   The dissents also argue that the claim in the instant case is barred by the doctrine of claim preclusion (also known as *res judicata*) because the issue was previously litigated in the *Abbott* case, which is cited in the excerpt above. In *Abbott* the plaintiffs, some of whom are also plaintiffs in the instant case, raised a facial attack on the admitting privileges provision of H.B. 2 before it was enforced. The plaintiffs lost on the merits in the Fifth Circuit and did not seek review in the Supreme Court. In this case, the plaintiffs raised an as-applied attack on the same statute, based on facts that arose subsequent to the enforcement of the statute. The Court found that the new claim that the admitting privileges requirement violated the Constitution, as applied, was not barred by the previous claim, and explained:

> When individuals claim that a particular statute will produce serious constitutionally relevant adverse consequences before they have occurred—and when courts doubt their occurrence—the factual difference that those adverse consequences *have actually occurred* can make all the difference. (emphasis in the original)

7.   The Court also found that the challenge to the surgical-center provision was not barred, despite the argument that it should have been brought with the earlier facial attack on the admitting-privileges requirement because both were part of the same statute and the same regulatory scheme, and thus arose out of the same transaction. As the Court pointed out:

> The surgical-center provision and the admitting-privileges provision are separate, distinct provisions of H.B. 2. They set forth two different, independent requirements with independent enforcement dates. This Court has never suggested that challenges to two different statutory provisions that serve two different functions must be brought in a single suit.

Although the Court rejected the claim preclusion defense, Justice Alito concluded that a contrary position was so obvious that Rule 11 sanctions could have been considered against the plaintiffs in the instant case. What does your knowledge of Civil Procedure tell you about the application of the claim preclusion doctrine here? If the Justices of the Supreme Court can disagree about its application with such absolute certainty in their righteousness, how are law students supposed to be able to apply it in their Civil Procedure classes?

8.   What is next for the pro-life movement, which has been active in seeking state legislation which it says is designed to protect women's health, over the next few years? Is the goal a different kind of state legislation or state legislation justified in other ways? Is the goal to work with legislatures to help them better articulate the purposes of their statutes that may limit access to abortion? Might the pro-life movement now return its attention to federal legislation, and, perhaps, the promulgation of a Constitutional amendment designed to eliminate any federal Constitutional right to an abortion? What is next for the pro-choice movement? Can it depend upon the five Justices in the

majority, which will remain a majority no matter who is appointed to replace the late Justice Scalia?

IV. ASSISTED REPRODUCTIVE TECHNOLOGIES (ART)

D. NATURAL AND GESTATIONAL SURROGACY

Add at page 1415, at the end of Note 2:

The parenting rights of same sex couples were established in *Obergefell v. Hodges*, 135 S.Ct. 2584 (2015), which found that denying the right to marry to same sex couples violated the Fourteenth Amendment. *Obergefell* provides that a state cannot treat married couples differently because of the sexual identity or preference of the spouses. Before *Obergefell* a dozen states limited the opportunity of same sex couples to adopt or foster children. In 2016 Mississippi, the last state to maintain such a statutory or regulatory limitation, saw it overturned by judicial decision. In granting a preliminary injunction against the Mississippi statute that prohibited adoption by same sex couples in Campaign for Southern Equality v. Miss. Dept. of Human Services, No. 3:15CV578-DPJ-FKB, 2016 WL 1306202 (S.D. Miss. Mar. 31, 2016), the judge evaluated the impact of *Obergefell* on adoptions:

> *Obergefell* held that bans on gay marriage violate the due-process and equal-protection clauses. It is the equal-protection component of the opinion that is relevant in the present dispute over Mississippi's ban on gay adoptions. Under traditional equal-protection analysis, a law that does not "target[ ] a suspect class" or involve a fundamental right will be upheld, "so long as it bears a rational relation to some legitimate end." [ ] Conversely, "if a classification does target a suspect class or impact a fundamental right, it will be strictly scrutinized and upheld only if it is precisely tailored to further a compelling government interest." [ ]

> In this case, Defendants argue that rational-basis review applies. But *Obergefell* made no reference to that or any other test in its equal-protection analysis. That omission must have been consciously made given the Chief Justice's full-throated dissent. [ ] ("Absent from this portion of the opinion, however, is anything resembling our usual framework for deciding equal protection cases . . . .").

> While the majority's approach could cause confusion if applied in lower courts to future cases involving marriage-related benefits, it evidences the majority's intent for sweeping change. For example, the majority clearly holds that marriage itself is a fundamental right when addressing the due-process issue. [ ] In the equal-protection context, that would require strict scrutiny. But the opinion also addresses the benefits of marriage, noting that marriage and those

varied rights associated with it are recognized as a "unified whole." [ ] And it further states that "the marriage laws enforced by the respondents are in essence unequal: same-sex couples are denied all the benefits afforded to opposite-sex couples and are barred from exercising a fundamental right." [ ]

Of course the Court did not state whether these other benefits are fundamental rights or whether gays are a suspect class. Had the classification not been suspect and the benefits not fundamental, then rational-basis review would have followed. It did not. Instead, it seems clear the Court applied something greater than rational-basis review. Indeed, the majority never discusses the states' reasons for adopting their bans on gay marriage and never mentions the word "rational."

While it may be hard to discern a precise test, the Court extended its holding to marriage-related benefits—which includes the right to adopt. And it did so despite those who urged restraint while marriage-related-benefits cases worked their way through the lower courts. According to the majority, "Were the Court to stay its hand to allow slower, case-by-case determination of the required availability of specific public benefits to same-sex couples, it still would deny gays and lesbians many rights and responsibilities intertwined with marriage." [ ]

* * *

In sum, the majority opinion foreclosed litigation over laws interfering with the right to marry and "rights and responsibilities intertwined with marriage." [ ] It also seems highly unlikely that the same court that held a state cannot ban gay marriage because it would deny benefits—expressly including the right to adopt—would then conclude that married gay couples can be denied that very same benefit.

While all states now must treat all married couples in the same way with regard to adoption, some states still find ways to impede the opportunity for gay or lesbian couples to develop families. In 2015, for example, Michigan provided that religious groups that contract with the state to do adoption placement can follow their own religious and ethical principles in making placements, even if that has the effect of avoiding placements with same sex couples. Other states have placed administrative burdens on those seeking to adopt, and some states have yet to revise their approach to the placement of foster children. There will be more litigation ahead to determine the limits on states' authority to use policy to encourage or facilitate discrimination against same sex couples with regard to adoption.

At page 1415, replace Note 3 with the following:

3.   In fact, a handful of states do permit a child to have more than two legally recognized parents, at least under some circumstances. For example,

after a California statutory change that became effective in 2014, a court can recognize that a child has more than two parents, but only where, according to the preface to the statute, such a finding "is necessary to protect the child from the detriment of being separated from one of his or her parents." More-than-two-parent-families are permitted but not preferred, it seems, under the judicial considerations required by the statute:

> In an appropriate action, a court may find that more than two persons with a claim to parentage under this division are parents if the court finds that recognizing only two parents would be detrimental to the child. In determining detriment to the child, the court shall consider all relevant factors, including, but not limited to, the harm of removing the child from a stable placement with a parent who has fulfilled the child's physical needs and the child's psychological needs for care and affection, and who has assumed that role for a substantial period of time. A finding of detriment to the child does not require a finding of unfitness of any of the parents or persons with a claim to parentage.

Ca. Fam. Code, § 7612(c). A handful of other states have also recognized more-than-two-parent families, either by statute or by judicial determination.

CHAPTER 16

LEGAL ISSUES IN HUMAN GENETICS

■ ■ ■

II. LEGAL RESPONSES

A. DISCRIMINATION BASED ON GENETIC INFORMATION

Add at page 1461 at the end of the note on The Federal Genetic Nondiscrimination Act of 2008 ("GINA"):

The broad definition of "genetic information" in GINA might appear to make impossible the implementation of some kinds of employee wellness programs specifically permitted by the Affordable Care Act. Specifically, asking employees and their spouses to provide answers to "voluntary" health risk assessment questionnaires, which was anticipated as part of wellness programs under the Affordable Care Act, would require those employees and spouses to give employers information about their past or current health status, which would include "the manifestation of a disease or disorder in family members of an individual." Any information about such a manifestation, however, is defined as genetic information in GINA, and thus it cannot be requested by the employer unless it fits within an exception for those employers offering their employees "voluntary" health services.

On May 17, 2016, the Equal Employment Opportunity Commission, which is charged with enforcing the employment provisions of GINA, issued a final rule attempting to harmonize the provisions of GINA and the ACA. It allows for the use of such health risk assessments, which can be tied to incentives (either positive incentives or penalties) as substantial as 30% of the cost of the employee's health plan, as long as the wellness programs are "reasonably well designed." They are reasonably well designed if they are designed to promote health or prevent disease, they are not overly burdensome for employees, they are not designed to get around GINA, and they are implemented for some reason other than merely shifting the cost of health coverage from the employer to the employee. Note that under the ACA and the EEOC final rule employers may request health status from employees and from their spouses, but not from their children.

For a view of this new rule from the perspective of the ACA, see the note in this Supplement that has been added to Chapter 9, Private Health Insurance and Managed Care: Liability and State and Federal Regulation, Section VI, Insurance Regulation Under the Affordable Care Act, Subsection A, Underwriting Reforms, added to page 669 of the casebook. See also Amendments to Regulations Under the Genetic Information Nondiscrimination Act of 2008, 81 Fed.Reg. 31143 (May 17, 2016), codified at 29 CFR § 1635.

C. NEWBORN GENETIC SCREENING

Add at page 1480 at the end of Note 1:

The Newborn Screen Saves Lives Reauthorization Act of 2014, P.L. 113–240, 128 Stat. 2851, which went into effect in March of 2015, provides explicitly that "[r]esearch on newborn dried blood spots shall be considered research carried out on human subjects" for purposes of federal regulation of research. Thus, federally funded research using those blood spots requires parental consent. The statute, which instructs the relevant federal agencies to incorporate this policy into regulations governing the use of human subjects by the end of 2016, also provides that the requirement of parental consent cannot be waived by the IRB in these cases. See the Act, section 12.

CHAPTER 17

ORGAN TRANSPLANTATION AND THE DETERMINATION OF DEATH

∎ ∎ ∎

II. ORGAN TRANSPLANTATION

C. LEGAL FRAMEWORK FOR THE PROCUREMENT OF ORGANS AND TISSUE FOR TRANSPLANTATION

3. Paying "Donors" for Organs and Tissue

Add at page 1508 at the end of Note 1:

After the decision in *Flynn v. Holder*, HHS issued a proposed regulation that would include in the definition of human organ "bone marrow and other hematopoietic stem/progenitor cells without regard to the method of their collection." 78 Fed. Reg. 60810 (Oct. 2, 2013). No Final Rule has been issued with this amendment as of the writing of this supplement.

III. THE DETERMINATION OF DEATH

C. THE DEAD DONOR RULE AND THE DETERMINATION OF DEATH

Add at page 1517 at the bottom:

IN RE GUARDIANSHIP OF HAILU
Supreme Court of Nevada, 2015.
361 P.3d 524.

PICKERING, J.:

"For legal and medical purposes, a person is dead if the person has sustained an irreversible cessation of . . . [a]ll functions of the person's entire brain, including his or her brain stem." NRS 451.007(1). The determination of death "must be made in accordance with accepted medical standards." NRS 451.007(2). Here, we are asked to decide whether the American Association of Neurology guidelines are considered "accepted medical standards" that satisfy the definition of brain death in NRS 451.007. We conclude that the district court failed to properly consider whether the American Association of Neurology guidelines adequately measure all functions of the entire brain, including the brain stem, . . . and are considered accepted medical standards by states that have adopted the Uniform Determination of Death Act. Accordingly, we reverse the district court's order denying a petition for temporary restraining order and remand.

FACTS

Medical history

On April 1, 2015, 20-year-old university student Aden Hailu went to St. Mary's Regional Medical Center (St. Mary's) after experiencing abdominal pain. Medical staff could not determine the cause of her pain and decided to perform an exploratory laparotomy and remove her appendix. During the laparotomy, Hailu's blood pressure was low and she suffered "severe, catastrophic anoxic, or lack of brain oxygen damage," and she never woke up. After her surgery, Hailu was transferred to the St. Mary's Intensive Care Unit (ICU), under the care of Dr. Anthony Floreani. Within the first two weeks of April, three different electroencephalogram (EEG) tests were conducted, all of which showed brain functioning.

On April 13, 2015, Dr. Aaron Heide, the Director of Neurology and Stroke at St. Mary's, first examined Hailu. Dr. Heide concluded that Hailu was not brain dead at that time but was "rapidly declining." To make that determination, Dr. Heide conducted an examination of Hailu's neurological functions; her left eye was minimally responsive, she was chewing on the ventilator tube, and she moved her arms with stimulation. The next day, April 14, 2015, Hailu did not exhibit these same indicia of neurological functioning.

On May 28, 2015, St. Mary's performed an apnea test, which involved taking Hailu off ventilation support for ten minutes to see if she could breathe on her own; Hailu failed the apnea test, leading St. Mary's to conclude that "[t]his test result confirms Brain Death unequivocally." Based on Hailu's condition, Dr. Jeffrey Bacon wrote the following in his notes: "Awaiting administration and hospital lawyers for direction re care—withdrawal of Ventilator support indicated NOW in my opinion as brain death unequivocally confirmed." On June 2, 2015, St. Mary's notified Hailu's father and guardian, Fanuel Gebreyes, that it intended to discontinue Hailu's ventilator and other life support. Gebreyes opposed taking Hailu off life support and sought judicial relief.

Procedural history

Gebreyes filed an emergency motion for temporary restraining order to enjoin St. Mary's from removing Hailu from life-sustaining services. On June 18, 2015, the district court held a hearing on the matter. The parties stipulated that St. Mary's would continue life-sustaining services until July 2, 2015, at 5:00 p.m. to allow Gebreyes to have an independent neurologist examine Hailu. They further stipulated that if, after the independent examination, Gebreyes wished St. Mary's to continue life support, he would need to request it through guardianship court. However, "if on July 2, 2015, it is determined that Aden Hailu is legally and clinically deceased, the hospital shall proceed as they see fit." Based on the stipulation, the district court dismissed the complaint for a temporary restraining order.

For reasons unknown, Gebreyes was unable to obtain the services of a neurologist before the stipulated July 2, 2015, deadline. Consequently, on July 1, 2015, Gebreyes filed an "Emergency Petition for Order Authorizing Medical Care, Restraining Order and Permanent Injunction." In the petition, he alleged that the doctors at St. Mary's had prematurely determined that Hailu had experienced brain death and sought to prevent the hospital from removing Hailu from the ventilator. St. Mary's opposed the emergency petition on July 2, 2015, and the district court held a hearing that same day.

At the July 2, 2015, hearing, the district court heard from four witnesses. First, Gebreyes testified that he wanted Hailu to get a tracheostomy and feeding tube to prepare her for transport; he hoped to take her home or relocate her to Las Vegas, where he resides. When asked why he did not obtain the services of another doctor to perform the tracheostomy, he stated that it was something he thought St. Mary's had to do because Hailu is at St. Mary's. Second, Gebreyes obtained the services of Dr. Paul Byrne—a known opponent of brain-death declarations who is unlicensed in Nevada—to testify that Hailu is still alive. Dr. Byrne complained that Hailu was never treated for thyroid problems and testified that this treatment will help her improve.

Third, Dr. Aaron Heide testified on behalf of St. Mary's. Dr. Heide applied the American Association of Neurology (AAN) guidelines to Hailu to determine if she was brain dead. He testified that the AAN guidelines are the accepted medical standard in Nevada. The AAN guidelines call for three determinations: (1) whether there is a coma and unresponsiveness; (2) whether there is brainstem activity (determined by conducting a clinical examination of reflexes, eyes, ears, etc.); and (3) whether the patient can breathe on her own (determined by conducting an apnea test). Although another doctor conducted the apnea test one month after Dr. Heide's last examination of Hailu, Dr. Heide believed that Hailu "had zero percent chance of any form of functional neurological outcome." Further, Dr. Heide also administered a Transcranial Doppler test, which is a test that measures blood flow to the brain. While there was still some blood flow to Hailu's brain, the lack of blood flow was consistent with brain death.

Last, Helen Lidholm, the CEO of St. Mary's, testified that the hospital is in favor of allowing Hailu to be transported to Las Vegas, where her father lives. Lidholm stated that St. Mary's "could make that happen" as long as Gebreyes arranges the proper medical equipment and transportation for Hailu and ensures a transfer location that can care for her. St. Mary's would allow the family to retain the services of any neurologist to come in and test Hailu as long as the physician is licensed in the State of Nevada; St. Mary's also offered to pay for the physician's examination fee. On cross-examination, Lidholm clarified that if the family has a licensed neurologist examine Hailu and determine that she is still alive, the physician can then order treatment for Hailu. Gebreyes said that he never received this offer before the hearing.

After Gebreyes said that he wanted to take advantage of the opportunity to bring in his own neurologist, the parties stipulated to extend the hearing until July 21, 2015, to give Gebreyes time to retain the services of a neurologist. The district court gave Gebreyes specific instructions on the care plan he must bring back to the court. First, the district court stated that Gebreyes needs a neurological expert because the matter involves "primarily neurological issues." Second, the care plan must determine "whether or not that physician is going to treat the patient, prescribe the protocol for the patient that the guardian is hoping for, and works with the guardian to accommodate transfer." Third, the plan must also include the method and manner of transportation, the new location, and the plan of care at the new location, along with the method of payment for such care. Finally, the care plan must be supported by medical evidence. Based on this stipulation, the district court continued the hearing to July 21, 2015.

On July 21, 2015, Gebreyes presented a plan to transport Hailu to Las Vegas based on the testimony of two physicians. First, Gebreyes called Dr. Brian Callister to testify. Dr. Callister is not a neurologist, but specializes in internal medicine and hospitalist medicine. He examined Hailu the day of his testimony and reviewed her medical records. Based on his examination of Hailu and review of her records, Dr. Callister testified: "I believe that her status is quite grim. I think that her chance of survival, her chance of awakening from her current state is a long shot. However, I do not think that the chance is zero." Dr. Callister stated that all three EEG tests did show brainwaves, albeit abnormal and slow. In Dr. Callister's opinion, the EEG tests are "something that should give you just enough pause to say you can't say with certainty that her chances are zero." Although Dr. Callister admitted that under the AAN guidelines Hailu's condition looks irreversible, Dr. Callister pointed to other factors that demonstrate improvement is a possibility. As examples, Dr. Callister cites Hailu's young age, her health, her skin, her ability to make urine and pass bowel movements, and the fact that the general functioning of the rest of her body is good. He explained that typically, someone kept alive by a ventilator shows other signs of deterioration, such as organ failures or necrosis of the hands and feet, that Hailu does not exhibit.

Finally, Dr. Callister questioned the reliability of the AAN guidelines stating that the AAN guidelines will always yield results consistent with brain death for a patient with a nonfunctioning cortex, even if the mid or hind parts of the brain are still functioning. Nevertheless, on cross-examination, Dr. Callister conceded that under "a strict definition" of the AAN guidelines, Hailu "would meet their category [of brain death]." On redirect, Dr. Callister concluded that "there's enough variables and enough questions based on the condition of her physical body, the EEG's and the fact that no further neurological testing has been done in several months, and the fact that no outside third party neurologist has looked at her that I would have pause."

* * *

Next, St. Mary's called Dr. Anthony Floreani to testify. Dr. Floreani took care of Hailu in the ICU since the night following her surgery. Dr. Floreani is a pulmonary doctor, not a neurologist. Dr. Floreani agreed with the conclusions of Dr. Heide that Hailu is brain dead. . . . Dr. Floreani testified that the St. Mary's doctors did the tests "by the book exactly how you should do it." Based on all of the evidence from the July 2 hearing and the July 21 hearing, the district court ruled in favor of St. Mary's. The district court stated that a restraining order should not be granted because the medical evidence from Dr. Heide and Dr. Floreani suggested that the AAN guidelines were followed, and thus, "medical standards were met, the outcome and criteria were satisfied in terms of the statute, the [AAN] protocol was followed, the outcome of the various three step tests under the [AAN] protocol all direct certification of death, and I agree." Despite ruling in St. Mary's favor, the district court granted an injunction pending Gebreyes's appeal to this court. The district court's written order was filed on July 30, 2015. Gebreyes appealed on August 3, 2015, and this court issued a stay of the district court's order and directed St. Mary's not to terminate Hailu's life-support systems pending resolution of the appeal. . . .

DISCUSSION

* * *

. . . [T]he statutory requirements of Nevada's Determination of Death Act that death be determined using "accepted medical standards" and that the Act be applied and construed in a manner "uniform among the states which enact it," [ ] necessitates a legal analysis regarding what the accepted medical standards are across the country. . . .

* * *

The district court focused exclusively on whether St. Mary's physicians satisfied the AAN guidelines, without discussing whether the AAN guidelines satisfy NRS 451.007. Although St. Mary's presented testimony that the AAN guidelines are the accepted medical standard in Nevada—albeit a simple "yes" to the question of whether the AAN guidelines are the accepted medical standard in Nevada—the district court and St. Mary's failed to demonstrate that the AAN guidelines are considered "accepted medical standards" that are applied uniformly throughout states that have enacted the UDDA as sufficient to meet the UDDA definition of brain death. The district court did not reach this issue at all, while St. Mary's has only cited one source to support its argument that the AAN guidelines are the nationally accepted medical standard.

St. Mary's cites the New Jersey Law Revision Commission's Report relating to the Declaration of Death Act. However, the report actually supports the opposite conclusion for which St. Mary's argues. In the report, New Jersey decided *against* adopting the AAN guidelines, stating that the AAN guidelines "are not uniformly accepted in the national (or even international) medical community." *See* N.J. Law Revision Comm'n, Final Report Relating to New Jersey Declaration of Death Act, at 14 (Jan. 18, 2013). Further, the report cited to multiple studies suggesting that "the AAN guidelines need more research" and "there is still a great variety of practice in U.S. hospitals" even though the AAN guidelines were published in 1995. Despite recognizing the AAN as guidelines "upon which most hospitals and physicians rely," the report concluded that the AAN guidelines were not so broadly adopted and utilized as to have become *the* accepted medical standard for determining brain death. Based on the foregoing, and the record before us, we are not convinced that the AAN guidelines are considered the accepted medical standard that can be applied in a way to make Nevada's Determination of Death Act uniform with states that have adopted it, as the UDDA requires. NRS 451.007(3) (recognizing that the purpose of adopting the UDDA in Nevada "is to make uniform among the states which enact it the law regarding the determination of death").

Contrarily, extensive case law demonstrates that at the time states began to adopt the UDDA, the uniformly accepted medical standard that existed was the then so-called Harvard criteria. The Harvard criteria require three steps, followed by a flat EEG as a confirmatory test: (1) unreceptivity and unresponsivity to painful stimuli; (2) no spontaneous movements or spontaneous respiration; and (3) no reflexes, as demonstrated by no ocular movement, no blinking, no swallowing, and fixed and dilated pupils. [ ]

It appears from a layperson's review of the Harvard criteria versus the AAN guidelines that the AAN guidelines incorporated many of the clinical tests used in the Harvard criteria. [ ] However, the AAN guidelines do not require confirmatory/ancillary testing, such as EEGs. Although the AAN guidelines state that ancillary testing should be ordered "only if clinical examination cannot be fully performed due to patient factors, or if apnea testing is inconclusive or aborted," the AAN's own study recognized that a decade after publication of the guidelines, 84 percent of brain death determinations still included EEG testing. [ ]

... We recognize the Legislature's broad definition of "accepted medical standards" to promote "the development and application of more sophisticated diagnostic methods." [ ] Therefore, we hesitate to limit the criteria to determine brain death "to a fixed point in the past." [ ]

Regrettably, however, the briefing and record before us do not answer two key questions. First, the briefing and testimony do not establish whether the AAN guidelines are considered accepted medical standards among states that have enacted the UDDA. Besides the single citation to the New Jersey Law Revision Commission Report, which as discussed above does not four-square support St. Mary's position, St. Mary's has failed to cite in its brief or during oral argument any medical or legal document that supports the AAN guidelines as accepted medical standards under the UDDA definition. Second, whatever their medical acceptance generally, the briefing and testimony do not establish whether the AAN guidelines adequately measure the extraordinarily broad standard laid out by NRS 451.007, which requires, before brain death can be declared under the UDDA, an "irreversible cessation" of "[a]*ll functions* of the person's *entire* brain, including his or her brain stem." [ ] Emphasis added. Though courts defer to the medical community to determine the applicable criteria to measure brain functioning, it is the duty of the law to establish the applicable standard that said criteria must meet. [ ] The record before us does not discuss whether the AAN guidelines require an irreversible cessation of all functions of a person's entire brain, including the brain stem, as NRS 451.007(1)(b) demands. ... Thus, we hold that the district court erred in denying Gebreyes's motion for a temporary restraining order.

* * *

We concur: HARDESTY, C.J., and PARRAGUIRRE, DOUGLAS, CHERRY, SAITTA, and GIBBONS, JJ.

NOTES AND QUESTIONS

1.   The Nevada Supreme Court remanded the case to the trial court for a determination of the central question. In subsequent proceedings, the hospital asked the trial court for permission to perform additional testing, including an EEG, over the father's objection, and the court allowed two EEGs to be performed. It's not clear whether that testing took place. Shortly before the date of the hearing on the issue of the remand, Aden Hailu suffered cardiopulmonary arrest. The death certificate listed the date of death as the date of the arrest. Siobhan McAndres, The Contested Death of Aden Hailu, Reno-Gazette-Journal, Mar. 25, 2016.

2.   The court is careful to note that it is not concluding that the AAN criteria are not the generally accepted medical standard for determining death, but only that the issue was not addressed in the court below. Does this concern seem to be primarily a formal requirement of specific consideration of the question, or is it more? It is clear from the court's discussion of the statute that it would accept only criteria that determined that there was absolutely no brain function. In a deleted footnote, the court cites several articles that point out that some function (specifically the hypothalamus) remains even in patients that are determined to be brain dead. See, e.g., Seema K. Shah, Piercing the Veil: The Limits of Brain Death as a Legal Fiction, 48 Mich. J. L. Reform 301 (2015). There is wide variability in the criteria used for determining brain death. See D.M. Greer, et al., Variability of Brain Death Policies in the U.S., 73 JAMA Neurology 213 (2016), documenting variations in a survey of hospital policies and advocating adoption of the AAN guidelines. Is the court dealing with a case where the medical standard is simply evolving and practitioners have not adopted newer standards, or is the court calling for testing that meets the literal standard of the cessation of all functions of the entire brain? If you were briefing the case for the trial court on remand in favor of the hospital, how would you handle the issue of variability among hospitals?

CHAPTER 19

MEDICALLY ASSISTED DYING

■ ■ ■

III. LEGISLATION TO SUPPORT MEDICALLY ASSISTED DYING—"DEATH WITH DIGNITY" INITIATIVES

At page 1717, replace Oregon Department of Human Services, Oregon's Death With Dignity Act—2012 with the following:

There was a substantial increase in the number of prescriptions written in Oregon in 2015, and the data (including that from the most recent years) is included in:

OREGON PUBLIC HEALTH DIVISION, OREGON'S DEATH WITH DIGNITY ACT—2015 DATA SUMMARY
(released February 4, 2016)

Introduction

Oregon's Death with Dignity Act (DWDA), enacted in late 1997, allows terminally-ill adult Oregonians to obtain and use prescriptions from their physicians for self-administered, lethal doses of medications.

The Oregon Public Health Division is required by the DWDA to collect compliance information and to issue an annual report. Data presented in this summary, including the number of people for whom DWDA prescriptions were written (DWDA prescription recipients) and the resulting deaths from the ingestion of the medications (DWDA deaths), are based on required reporting forms and death certificates received by the Oregon Public Health Division as of January 27, 2016. More information on the reporting process, required forms, and annual reports is available at: http://www.healthoregon.org/dwd.

Participation Summary and Trends

During 2015, 218 people received prescriptions for lethal medications under the provisions of the Oregon DWDA, compared to 155 during 2014 (Figure 1, above). As of January 27, 2016, the Oregon Public Health Division had received reports of 132 people who had died during 2015 from ingesting the medications prescribed under DWDA.

Since the law was passed in 1997, a total of 1,545 people have had prescriptions written under the DWDA, and 991 patients have died from ingesting the medications. From 1998 through 2013, the number of prescriptions written annually increased at an average of 12.1%; however, during 2014 and 2015, the number of prescriptions written increased by an average of 24.4%. During 2015, the rate of DWDA deaths was 38.6 per 10,000 total deaths.

* * * Of the 218 patients for whom prescriptions were written during 2015, 125 (57.3%) ingested the medication; all 125 patients died from ingesting the medication without regaining consciousness. Fifty of the 218 patients who received DWDA prescriptions during 2015 did not take the medications and subsequently died of other causes.

Ingestion status is unknown for 43 patients prescribed DWDA medications in 2015. Five of these patients died, but they were lost to follow-up or the follow-up questionnaires have not yet been received. For the remaining 38 patients, both death and ingestion status are pending [ ].

Patient Characteristics

Of the 132 DWDA deaths during 2015, most patients (78.0%) were aged 65 years or older. The median age at death was 73 years. As in previous years, decedents were commonly white (93.1%) and well educated (43.1% had a least a baccalaureate degree).

While most patients had cancer, the percent of patients with cancer in 2015 was slightly lower than in previous years (72.0% and 77.9%, respectively). The percent of patients with amyotrophic lateral sclerosis (ALS) was also lower (6.1% in 2015, compared to 8.3% in previous years). Heart disease increased from 2.0% in prior years to 6.8% in 2015.

Most (90.1%) patients died at home, and most (92.2%) were enrolled in hospice care. Excluding unknown cases, most (99.2%) had some form of health care insurance, although the percent of patients who had private insurance (36.7%) was lower in 2015 than in previous years (60.2%). The number of patients who had only Medicare or Medicaid insurance was higher than in previous years (62.5% compared to 38.3%).

Similar to previous years, the three most frequently mentioned end-of-life concerns were: decreasing ability to participate in activities that made life enjoyable (96.2%), loss of autonomy (92.4%), and loss of dignity (75.4%).

DWDA Process

A total of 106 physicians wrote 218 prescriptions during 2015 (1-27 prescriptions per physician). During 2015, no referrals were made to the Oregon Medical Board for failure to comply with DWDA requirements.

During 2015, five patients were referred for psychological/ psychiatric evaluation.

A procedure revision was made in 2010 to standardize reporting on the follow-up questionnaire. The new procedure accepts information about the time of death and circumstances surrounding death only when the physician or another health care provider was present at the time of death. For 27 patients, either the prescribing physician or another healthcare provider was present at the time of death.

Prescribing physicians were present at time of death for 14 patients (10.8%) during 2015 compared to 15.7% in previous years; 13 additional cases had other health care providers present (e.g. hospice nurse). Data on time from ingestion to death is available for only 25 DWDA deaths during 2015. Among those 25 patients, time from ingestion until death ranged from five minutes to 34 hours. For the remaining two patients, the length of time between ingestion and death was unknown.

For the full text of this report, and substantial additional data, see https://public.health.oregon.gov/ProviderPartnerResources/Evaluation Research/DeathwithDignityAct/Documents/year18.pdf.

Add at page 1722 after Note 8:

In 2015 California became the fifth state to allow medically assisted dying (now almost universally called "aid in dying") under some circumstances. The California End of Life Option Act, Cal. Health & Safety Code sec. 443 et seq., became effective in June of 2016. Enacted after the very high profile death of Brittany Maynard, a young and articulate brain cancer patient who was forced to move from California to Oregon to avail herself of aid in dying, the End of Life Option Act is modeled on the Oregon Death with Dignity Act and varies from it in just a few relatively insignificant ways. The California Medical Association gave a big boost to the End of Life Option Act when it retracted its opposition to aid in dying and announced it was neutral with regard to the bill.

The California law, unlike the Oregon law, requires that the prescribing physician speak privately with the patient before prescribing a lethal dose to assure that the patient is not being pressured into seeking the prescription. It also specifically provides for the use of an interpreter for those who do not speak English, provides for the disposal of any leftover medication, and provides a form to be filled out by the patient sometime during the 48-hour period before the medication is consumed. The last requirement is hardly enforceable, of course; there is no recourse against someone who successfully ingests the medication. For the full text of the statute, a summary of its provisions, a legislative history, and an account of the policies promulgated by individual institutions as the law went into effect, see http://www. ucconsortium.org/portfolio-view/end-of-life-care-act-fact-sheet/.

There has been considerable debate over what would constitute an appropriate institutional policy to carry out the California legislation. The statute permits any institutional or individual provider to opt out of providing aid in dying, and many providers—including, perhaps, all Catholic institutions—have opted out. Some secular hospitals have also opted out, either because of ethical unease or risk management unease, or a combination of the two. At least one big state university medical center has adopted a policy requiring that anyone seeking aid in dying be referred for a mental status examination and determination of competence. That institution, on one extreme of the risk management spectrum, prohibits patients from taking the prescribed lethal dose on the medical center campus, and also provides that no prescription be written for a patient who comes to the institution only for the purpose of obtaining the prescription. If an institution can opt out of aid in dying all together, can it also put any condition it wishes on providing it? Can a state institution (like a state run university medical school) decide, as a matter of policy, not to make available a treatment alternative explicitly allowed by statute?

There has been a host of litigation surrounding aid in dying in California. Before the End of Life Option Act went into effect there were at least two state constitutional challenges to the statute criminalizing aid in dying as assisted suicide. Both failed as the trial courts and two California Court of Appeal panels decided that the issue was one properly left to the legislature, which could decide whether to permit aid in dying, and under what circumstances. Near the effective date of the statute, opponents of aid in dying sought an injunction against the statute, arguing that the statute violated the equal protection clause of the federal and state constitutions because it left terminally ill patients, unlike others, without the protection offered by the assisted suicide statute. The trial court denied the application for a temporary restraining order in that case; the hearing on the preliminary injunction was pending when this Supplement went to press.

A separate attempt to stop the End of Life Option Act from going into effect through referendum—a direct vote of the people to effectively veto the act of the legislature—failed when supporters could not get the necessary number of signatures to put the measure on the ballot.

Litigation designed to recognize a state constitutional right to aid in dying failed in 2015 and 2016 in Kentucky, New York and New Mexico as well as in California (where the issue was subsequently resolved by the statute described above). As a general matter, advocates of aid in dying have turned from state constitutional litigation, which has been successful only in Montana, to legislation and political activity. A measure to allow Aid in Dying has qualified for the ballot in Colorado, and in November 2016 the voters of that state will decide whether to become the sixth state to permit it.

At page 1724, replace the last paragraph of Note 11 with the following:

Litigation was more successful in Canada, where the Supreme Court decided that it would be a violation of Canada's Charter of Rights to apply the criminal law against aiding and abetting suicide to a physician who helps end the life of a "competent adult person * * * who clearly consents to the termination of life" and who "has a grievous and irremediable medical condition (including an illness, disease, or disability) that causes enduring suffering that is intolerable to the individual in the circumstances of his or her condition." *Carter v. Canada (Attorney General)*, 2015 SCC 5 (Supreme Court of Canada, 2015). The Court gave the Parliament until February of 2016 (subsequently postponed until June of 2016) to devise an appropriate process and establish appropriate safeguards for such intervention through the legislative process. In June of 2016 the Parliament promulgated Bill C-14, formally authorizing physician participation in the death of patients under some circumstances. Although the *Carter* decision did not require that the person requesting aid from a physician be terminally ill (as is the case in every state in the United States that allows aid in dying), the statute added a requirement that the patient's natural death be "reasonably foreseeable." Some advocates for aid in dying believe that this legislative back-door requirement that the patient be terminal violates the principles underlying *Carter*, and it is likely to be challenged in the Canadian courts by those with chronic illnesses who suffer grievous medical conditions they find intolerable and who seek physician assistance in their deaths, but whose deaths are *not* reasonably foreseeable.

In addition to the fact that Canadian law has a much more flexible terminal illness requirement than those in the United States, Canadian law is different from the Oregon-like model in that it permits both traditional aid in dying (a physician writing a lethal prescription for medication to be ingested by the patient) and also direct action by a physician to cause the death of a patient (for example, a physician giving a lethal injection). Essentially, it allows for euthanasia as well as aid in dying. Before June of 2016 euthanasia was available only in Belgium, the Netherlands and Luxembourg.

Add at page 1724 after the last paragraph of Note 11:

SPECIAL BIBLIOGRAPHIC NOTE

There is a tremendous amount of current and useful legal and medical information on aid in dying and related processes, and a wonderful collection of cited sources, in a new article that is worth reading despite the preconceptions of the authors betrayed in their choice of the terms "euthanasia" and "physician-assisted suicide" in the title. See E. Emanuel, B. Onwuteaka-Philipsen, J. Urwin and J. Cohen, Attitudes and Practices of Euthanasia and Physician-Assisted Suicide in the United States, Canada and Europe, 316(1) JAMA 79–90 (July 5, 2016). In fact, much of the July 5, 2016 JAMA is dedicated to subjects related to end of life care and end of life policy; you will find it an extremely useful issue if you have an interest in that area.

CHAPTER 20

REGULATION OF RESEARCH INVOLVING HUMAN SUBJECTS

■ ■ ■

III. FEDERAL REGULATION OF RESEARCH

B. REVISION OF THE FEDERAL REGULATIONS

Add at page 1762 as new Note 4:

4.   Each of the federal agencies who ascribe to the Common Rule participated in issuing a Notice of Proposed Rulemaking (NPRM) as a follow up to the ANPRM. 80 Fed. Reg. 53933 (Sept. 8, 2015). The comment period for the proposed regulations closed in January 2016, and final regulations have not been promulgated as of the date on which this supplement was written. The NPRM identifies the most significant changes to the current regulations:

(1) Improve informed consent by increasing transparency and by imposing stricter new requirements regarding the information that must be given to prospective subjects, and the manner in which it is given to them, to better assure that subjects are appropriately informed before they decide to enroll in a research study.

(2) Generally require informed consent for the use of stored biospecimens in secondary research (for example, part of a blood sample that is left over after being drawn for clinical purposes), even if the investigator is not being given information that would enable him or her to identify whose biospecimen it is. That consent would generally be obtained by means of broad consent (i.e., consent for future, unspecified research studies) to the storage and eventual research use of biospecimens.

(3) Exclude from coverage under the Common Rule certain categories of activities that should be deemed not to be research, are inherently low risk, or where protections similar to those usually provided by IRB review are separately mandated.

(4) Add additional categories of exempt research to accommodate changes in the scientific landscape and to better calibrate the level of review to the level of risk involved in the research. A new process would allow studies to be determined to be exempt without requiring any administrative or IRB review. Certain exempt and all non-exempt research would be required to provide privacy safeguards for

biospecimens and identifiable private information. New categories include:

    a.   certain research involving benign interventions with adult subjects;

    b.   research involving educational tests, surveys, interviews or observations of public behavior when sensitive information may be collected, provided that data security and information privacy protections policies are followed;

    c.   secondary research use of identifiable private information originally collected as part of a non-research activity, where notice of such possible use was given;

    d.   storing or maintaining biospecimens and identifiable private information for future, unspecified secondary research studies, or conducting such studies, when a broad consent template to be promulgated by the Secretary of HHS is used, information and biospecimen privacy safeguards are followed, and limited IRB approval of the consent process used is obtained.

(5)   Change the conditions and requirements for waiver or alteration of consent such that waiver of consent for research involving biospecimens (regardless of identifiability) will occur only in very rare circumstances.

(6)   Mandate that U.S. institutions engaged in cooperative research rely on a single IRB for that portion of the research that takes place within the United States, with certain exceptions. To encourage the use of IRBs that are otherwise not affiliated with or operated by an assurance-holding institution ("unaffiliated IRBs"), this NPRM also includes a proposal that would hold such IRBs directly responsible for compliance with the Common Rule. [Ed. Note: This would not apply to research for FDA-approved devices or research conducted abroad.]

(7)   Eliminate the continuing review requirement for studies that undergo expedited review and for studies that have completed study interventions and are merely analyzing data or involve only observational follow-up in conjunction with standard clinical care.

(8)   Extend the scope of the policy to cover all clinical trials, regardless of funding source, conducted at a U.S. institution that receives federal funding for non-exempt human subjects research.

Specific changes between the ANPRM and the NPRM are noted below where appropriate.

IV. ENFORCEMENT STRUCTURE AND PROCESS

C. ENFORCEMENT BY PRIVATE LITIGATION

Add at page 1779 at the end of *Note: Research With Children*:

Many of the changes proposed in the NPRM to reduce the level of review and control over certain research protocols would not apply to research involving children.

V. APPLYING THE COMMON RULE

A. RESEARCH SUBJECT TO THE FEDERAL REGULATIONS

Add at page 1779 at the end of the second paragraph:

The NPRM extends the application of the federal regulations to all clinical trials, except those regulated by the FDA, conducted within an organization in the U.S. that receives funding for non-exempt or non-excluded research regardless of the source of funding of the specific research. See also Note 2 on Page 1776 of the casebook.

Add at page 1780 to the end of the first paragraph in *Problem: Is It Research?*:

The proposed regulations in the NPRM create a new category of "exclusions" to describe activities that are not subject to the regulations. It distinguishes these exclusions from the current category of exempt research. Exclusions are not subject to the regulations. The exclusions identified in the agencies' comments in the NPRM are judged to share certain characteristics. They are considered either not to be research at all; or if they are research their "contribution to public welfare is so imperative that they should proceed without having to satisfy the regulatory requirements;" or they are so low-risk and nonintrusive that regulatory protections are "an unnecessary use of time and resources" while "the potential benefits of the research are substantial." Applying the final characteristic, the NPRM proposes moving some currently exempt research into the exclusions. Also in the final group is research by a HIPAA "covered entity" using "protected health information" that is regulated by the HIPAA Privacy Rule. (See Chapter 4 page 268 of the casebook.) The exclusion does not apply to research performed by a non-covered entity even if the information was originally provided by a covered entity.

The NPRM identifies 11 types of activities that would not be subject to the federal regulations on research. The exclusions include two activities relevant to this Problem.

First, is the exclusion of data collection (through surveys) and analysis (using data or biospecimens collected for other purposes) for use in the organization's own internal quality improvement and performance monitoring. The NPRM contrasts two situations:

> An example of an activity that would satisfy this exclusion is a survey of hospital patients to evaluate and improve the quality of meals delivered to hospital patients. An example of an activity that would not satisfy this exclusion is a prospective observational study of patient treatments to analyze the comparative effectiveness of two different standard of care treatments frequently used to treat the same medical condition.

The second is the exclusion of "quality assurance and quality improvement" activities that test the effectiveness of different approaches to increasing compliance with accepted practices. The NPRM contrasts two situations:

> [A]ssume that there is an accepted practice that is known to reduce the likelihood of an infection after the insertion of a central line. A randomized study in which half the participating institutions would be assigned to have the staff undergo an educational intervention about the need to use that accepted practice, and the other half would not undergo that intervention, would satisfy this exclusion, since it would only be intended to see if the intervention resulted in greater use of the accepted practice. In contrast, imagine a different study that was designed to determine how well that accepted practice, when it is used, reduces infections. That study would not satisfy this exclusion, since it would be studying the effectiveness of the practice itself, in contrast to studying an effort to increase use of the practice.

C. RISK AND CONSENT

Add at page 1783 after the first paragraph:

The NPRM follows up on the promise of the ANPRM to significantly revise the management of the consent process but it does not propose a system for pre-approved or mandatory consent forms. Instead, the proposed rules emphasize the importance of communicating information that is relevant to the decision to participate and in a manner that is understandable. When biospecimens are used the proposed rule requires that a participant be informed that they may be used for commercially profitable purposes and whether the participant will share in that profit. The proposed rule requires that potential subjects be informed whether clinically relevant research results will be shared with the participant. See note for Page 1785 below. The NPRM proposes requiring that informed consent forms be posted on a publicly available federal web site within 60 days of the close of a research study. The NPRM also provides criteria for "broad consent" to be used in relation to studies of previously collected biospecimens. See note for Page 1799 below.

Add at page 1785 at the end of the last paragraph:

The NPRM addresses some of the issues relating to incidental findings in research. In its treatment of the use of previously collected data and biospecimens, for example, the proposed regulations allow such research on the basis of "broad consent" to unspecified future research rather than consent to specific research projects. If the researcher anticipates returning results to the individuals involved, however, the research would not be exempt and the NPRM requires that the IRB review the protocol and that informed consent from the individual for the specific research be secured. If return of individual results is not anticipated but is later desired by the researcher, the NPRM requires that the IRB review and approve the plan for returning results. The agencies' comments to the NPRM note that genetic studies will often produce clinically relevant health information that is not related to the specific purpose of the research. The NPRM does not create any obligations to return results or disclose such information if the consent forms are clear that such information will not be disclosed to participants. The NPRM notes, however, that HIPAA may give individuals the right to access certain personal health information, and that right continues in the context of research. The NPRM also notes that clinical care of the individual may require the timely return of results, which should be anticipated and included in IRB review of the protocol. The NPRM suggests that IRBs may not have the competencies to account for issues surrounding incidental findings and so asks for comments on whether a federal panel of experts should be developed.

D. COMMERCIALIZATION OF THE RESEARCH ENTERPRISE

Add at page 1792 as a new Note 4:

4. Proposed regulations require that potential research participants be informed, in the informed consent form, that their biospecimens may be used for commercially profitable purposes and whether they will share in those profits. The proposed rules do not prohibit commercial uses and do not require payment to the subjects.

E. TISSUE AND DATA BANKS

Add at page 1801 to Note 4:

The Newborn Screening Saves Lives Reauthorization Act of 2014 (P.L. 113–240) provides that research with newborn dried blood spots that is federally funded under the Public Health Service Act is to be considered research with human subjects, and the current provisions allowing IRBs to waive consent do not apply.

Add at page 1801 as new Notes 5 and 6:

5.   The ANPRM proposed to harmonize the definition of identifiability and requirements for deidentification as between HIPAA and the Common Rule. The NPRM, however, proposes maintaining the current Common Rule definition and requirements in response to comments arguing that the HIPAA standards significantly impeded research. As in the current regulations, consent would not be required for the use of deidentified health information.

The NPRM departs significantly from the current regulations and from the ANPRM on the use of data that has been collected for purposes other than the specific research project. Like the ANPRM, the NPRM treats data (as information) differently than it treats research on biospecimens. The NPRM moves research using identifiable private information into the category of exempt research. To be considered exempt, the research protocol must comply with the privacy standards of the proposed regulations, must include notice to the individuals whose information is used that their private information may be used in research, and must be confined to the research purpose for which the information was accessed. Consent is not required. (The current category of exempt research is described in 45 C.F.R. § 46.101(b) at page 1753 of the casebook. Although a research protocol may fit within the exempt category, IRBs typically do a brief review, often by administrative staff, to assure that it does. The NPRM proposes a structure to make practices regarding exempt studies more consistent and efficient.) The NPRM moves certain other activities using identifiable private information into the new category of "exclusions," which are activities that would no longer be subject to the federal regulations. See note for Page 1780 above for description of that category. The NPRM proposes alternative approaches to regulating the use of health information as well and asks for comments on those.

6.   The NPRM keeps the general framework for the use of biospecimens proposed in the ANPRM, including setting different standards for the use of biospecimens as compared to data. (See previous note above.) The NPRM does, however, provide for a delay in implementation of the new requirements for three years after the date of the promulgation of final regulations. The proposed rule allows some narrow research with stored biospecimens to be done without consent. The NPRM describes those situations as ones where the aim is not to generate new knowledge about the person but only to confirm what is known and includes development of diagnostic tests on tissue known to have the target disease and known not to; proficiency testing; and quality assurance and control activities. There are some narrow exceptions from the consent requirements, and IRBs can waive the consent requirement in very limited circumstances. The intense struggle over how best to govern the use of biospecimens in relation to consent is apparent in the NPRM. In addition to the proposed regulations, the NPRM offers two different alternative structures, which would reach a narrower subset of research with biospecimens, and asks for comments on those as well.

The NPRM provides very detailed requirements for the "broad consent" for future unspecified research required for the use of previously collected biospecimens. If a subject refuses broad consent, the IRB would not be permitted to waive consent requirements for subsequent research with those biospecimens.

The NPRM also categorizes the storage and maintenance of identifiable private information and biospecimens that have been collected for non-research purposes or for other research purposes as exempt to facilitate the aggregation of data and biospecimens. Written consent for storage and future use from the individuals whose information or specimens are included must be secured, and the IRB does a limited review. Secondary research use of these data banks must satisfy the requirements described above. These provisions do not apply to the process of acquiring new data or tissue from individuals.